TRIBUTE OF YU
AN EXPOSITION OF THE NINE ANCIENT PREFECTURES OF SINITIC CHINA

by

Hong Yuan

HONG YUAN

TRIBUTE OF YU
AN EXPOSITION OF THE NINE ANCIENT PREFECTURES OF SINITIC CHINA

ISBN: 979-8-6004-1547-8

This book *TRIBUTE OF YU* is part of the Series on "Ancient Epic, Divination, Cosmology, Mythogeography & Theology", including:

> *Heavenly Questions - An Ancient Chinese Epic with a Hybrid of Questions about the Riddles and Enigma Concerning the Universe, Genesis, Nature, and the Rise and Fall of Dynasties*

> *The Legends of Mountains & Seas - A Non-Bestiary Interpretation of Divination, Sorcery, Demigods, Gods, Religion, Immortality, Metamorphosis, Cosmology, Mythogeography and Folklore of Ancient China*

> *Tribute of Yu - An Exposition of the Nine Ancient Prefectures of Sinitic China*

> *Zhou King Muwang's Travels - A Fictional Dissection of Ancient China's Rendezvous with Queen Mother of the West*

TABLE OF CONTENTS

INTRODUCTION

Yu Gong (Lord Yu's Tributes; Tribute of Yu), which talked about Lord Yu's flood control and zoning of the nine prefectures of Sinitic China, was the cornerstone on which the Sinitic nation, with the three successive dynasties of Xia, Shang and Zhou from the same big family, was founded, and the blueprint according to which the imperial administrative layout was mapped throughout the past millennia. *Yu Gong* was purportedly a chapter among *Xia Shu* (book of the Xia dynasty) in the post-Confucius Confucian Classic *Shang-shu* (remotely ancient history; book of documents), that was seen in Sima Qian's *Shi-ji* (historian's records; historic records). It was taken to be a pseudepigrapha, i.e., written by Lord Yu (r. ? 2207-2198 BC per Lu Jinggui; ? 1989-1982 per the forgery bamboo annals) and his assistant Bo-yi during the era of flood-control, i.e., about 2200-2300 B.C.E. The book, however, could not have been written earlier than the Warring States time period (475-221 B.C.), and might not be part of Confucius' abridged *Shang-shu* commandments, oaths, mottos and promulgations from the three dynasties of Xia, Shang and Zhou for the contents' not conforming to the axiomatic nature of the texts that were repeatedly cited by the Zhou dynasty kings and vassalage lords as seen in the hardening-tested history annals *Zuo Zhuan*.

Yu Gong neither belonged to the forgery set of the ancient version *Shang-shu* that was submitted to the Eastern Jinn dynasty court by Mei Yi, a series of books written by Huangfu Mi but pretentiously attributed to the long-lost Kong An'guo-collected version from the double-walls of Confucius' mansion. In today's *Xia Shu* section of *Shang-shu*, there are only four chapters, including *Yu Gong, Gan Shi4* (oath of war at Gan), *Wu-zi Zhi Ge* (five brothers' songs), and *Yin4 Zheng* (minister Yin4's campaign), with *Wu-zi Zhi Ge* and *Yin4 Zheng* taken to be the forged "ancient" version while the other two chapters were taken to be the Han-dynasty contemporary or orally recited original texts. There were three non-original versions of *Shang-shu* according to the phases of time: i) Fu Sheng's orally-recited texts of the clerical-script *Shang-shu* in the early Han dynasty; ii) the tadpole-script trove of the ancient version *Shang-shu* that was discovered in the double walls of Confucius' residence; and iii) the extra 25 chapter forgery "ancient version *Shang-shu*" that was ascribed to Mei Yi, magistrate for the Yuzhang commandery of the Eastern Jinn dynasty. Among the latter would be a chapter called *Da-Yu Mo* [flood-quelling masterplan or admonition] in *Yu4 Shu* (Lord Shun's book) of *Shang-shu*. (Huangfu Mi, calling the 58 chapters of forgery ancient version *Shang-shu* as a guide, wrote his book *Di-wang Shi4-ji* (Book of the Lineages of the Thearchs and Kings), where could be found the forger fingerprints as to numerous ancient thearchs' birthdays and birthplaces.)

Lord Yu's flood quelling activity, which was touted in *Shi-jing* (Book of Poems), is corroborated by the *Sui4-gong Xu* bronzeware on which Yu's flood quelling activity was inscribed with words similar to *Yu Gong* (Lord Yu's Tributes). *Zuo Zhuan*, in Lu Lord Zhaogong's 12th year or 530 B.C., claimed that absent Lord Yu everybody would become fish in the water. Numerous ancient classics, such as *Li Zheng* of *Shang-shu*, repeatedly talked about 'Yu ji', i.e., Lord Yu's footprints. Some Shang bronzeware called *Xiang3 ru2* (offer to Ru2/Yu) was recently discovered in Hejin of Shanxi, talking about the Shang king's making sacrifice to Lord Yu. This was taken to be the oldest artifact proving Lord Yu and Xia dynasty's existence. Additionally, there are numerous pieces of bronzeware that specifically talked about Lord Yu's footsteps, such as *Qin-gong Gui* (Qin Lord Xianggong's 'gui' tureen vessel), and the high lord's overlooking the Xia land (i.e., 'nao'), such as *Shi-qiang Pan* bronzeware dated to King Gongwang (r. 946 - 935 B.C. per Liu Xin/Shao Yong; 951-929 B.C. per Zhang Wenyu; 907-896 per [forgery version] *The Bamboo Annals*; 922-900 B.C. per the gap reign year project)'s reign. (The caveat is that the original Xia people's land could be very much restricted to the You-Xia-zhi-ju land near today's Luoyang of Henan and on the southern bank of the Yellow River and that the famed nine prefectures could be actually the mountain area to the south of Luoyang and to the west of the Nanyang basin. This is an area eulogized by poem *Song Gao* (tall Songshan mountain) as at least three fiefs of the four ordained ministers for the four tall mountains of China, i.e., Shen-guo, Fuguo (i.e., Lv-guo), Qi and Xu3-guo states. Jacques Gernet took Hsia (Xia) as "very probable the existence of this dynasty" for the traces of "the first city-palaces and the first manifestations of Chinese civilization to the end of the third millennium", and further pointed out that the Shang dynasty and the earlier Lungshan (Longshan) Culture exhibited a direct succession, as represented in the "very typical shapes which appear in closely related versions both in the fine black pottery of Shantung (Lungshan) and in the bronze vessels of the Shang period".)

The Xia dynasty (? 2177-1746 B.C. per Huangfu Mi; 2169-1739 B.C. per Seng Yixing; 2224-1766 B.C. per Shao Yong; 1978-1559 B.C. from Qi to Jie per the forgery contemporary version of *The Bamboo Annals*) was called the first dynasty. Jacques Gernet took Hsia (Xia) as "very probable the existence of this dynasty" for the traces of "the first city-palaces and the first manifestations of Chinese civilization to the end of the third millennium", and further pointed out that the Shang dynasty and the earlier Lungshan (Longshan) Culture exhibited a direct succession". The Xia dynasty's first king was Qi3, i.e., son of Lord Yu. Lord Yu was the person famous for being the man who mastered the floods, with the flood control work starting from the point of 'ji-shi' (i.e., piled-up rocks) per *Yu Gong*, which was apparently at the intersection of the Eastern and Northern Yellow River Bends, where a Jishi-jun Military Circuit was established in the Tang dynasty time period. This is not the latter-day appropriated 'Ji-shi' Minor location near today's Lanzhou or 'Ji-shi' Major location in the Yellow River Nine Winding area.

Sinitic China's faded memory of the past, i.e., flood control at the piled-up rocks, actually proved the extent of the Yangshao

Culture's expansion towards today's Inner Mongolia belt. While Kunlun, or Ji-shi, was not seen in the Spring & Autumn time period, Sinitic China, on a grand scale, long ago talked about Lord Yu's footsteps across the land and the accomplishments of flood control that averted the fate of people becoming fish, and on a micro scale, talked about the nine ancient prefectures that were the mountain area south of the West-to-East flowing Yellow River –which implied that the Xia people had origin there before embarking on the nation-wide flood control work. (Jacques Gernet likened the central place of Mount Kunlun to Mount Sumeru, i.e., what Richard E. Strassberg claimed as *axis mundi* or pillar of the sky, not knowing that Kunlun had a much older denotation in *Yu Gong* as a tribe, not a mountain. Further, Kunlun was not taken to be the center of world or the centric paramount sky-propping pillar of the earth till the Han-Jinn dynasties. Note that Liu Xie (? 465-520 A.D.), in *Bian Sao* (collating *Li Sao* poem) of *Wen-xing Diao-long* (Literary Mind and Carved Dragons), a book of literary aesthetics, numerology and divination, claimed that Kunlun and Xuanpu (hanging gardens) were not carried by '*Jing* [five Confucian classics] *Yi* [*Zhou Yi/I Ching*, i.e., or *Book of Changes*]'.)

Yu Gong could be divided into five major sections: i) the nine prefectures, ii) the repair work on the mountains; iii) the channeling of the rivers; iv) the flood control feats; and v) the five tribute regions. In the section on the nine prefectures, the Sinitic land was divided into nine regions, with mountains and rivers used as dividers and markers. Inside of each and every prefecture, there was the same order and symmetrical description of details about the boundaries, the mountain ranges and the rivers, the survey work and the improvement works conducted by Lord Yu, the soils and their properties, the tributary classification, the tribes and people, and the geography and the passage to the lord's capital city [in Jizhou the centric prefecture], etc. The nine prefectures were: Jizhou, Yanzhou, Qingzhou, Xuzhou, Yangzhou, Jingzhou, Yuzhou, Liangzhou, and Yongzhou. (*You Shi* of *Lv-shi Chun-qiu* gave a slightly different list of nine prefectures, albeit in the same clockwise direction: Yuzhou, Jizhou, Yanzhou, Qing-zhou, Xuzhou, Yangzhou, Jingzhou, Yuzhou, Yongzhou and Liang-zhou. *Yi Zhou Shu*, which had to be later than *Yu Gong* and *Lv-shi Chun-qiu*, listed nine different prefectures as Jizhou, Yanzhou, Qingzhou, Yangzhou, Jingzhou, Yuzhou, Yongzhou, Youzhou, and Bingzhou.).

CHAPTER I TRIBUTE OF YU'S AGE OF AUTHORSHIP IN THE LATE WARRING STATES TIME PERIOD

Yu Gong (Lord Yu's Tributes, Tribute of Yu) was an article written by some unknown person in the late Warring States time period of the Zhou dynasty in the name of Lord Yu, i.e., founder-king of the Xia dynasty, with the last sentence stating that Lord Yu received the award of a black jade 'gui' ware [power instrument with a pointer and square base] from Lord Yao for completing the flood control project. Qu Yuan, in poem *Tian Wen* (asking heaven, heavenly questions), questioned as to how Lord Yu subdivided the nine prefectures. The book *Yu Gong* could have been written just prior to Zou Yan (Zou-zi, ? 305-240 B.C.)'s proposition of the nine greater prefectures and the modification of the ancient nine prefectures' concept into twelve prefectures seen in *Yao Dian* of *Shang-shu*.

Gu Jiegang believed that it was the Han dynasty people who invented the twelve prefectures' concept on basis of a *Zuo Zhuan* statement in Lu Lord Aigong's 7th year that twelve was the heaven's "large number", i.e., the Jupiter's years of revolution. The most likely case that the nine prefectures turned into the twelve prefectures could have something to do with the fad of '*fen ye*' [marked fields] divisions of the land under the heaven in accordance with the twelve sector divisions of the ecliptic, as seen in the classification of the Qin people or the Zhou people's land under the Yongzhou prefecture rather than the Liangzhou prefecture. The nine '*fen ye*' [marked fields] divisions of the land in *Lv-shi Chun-qiu* (Lv Buwei's spring & autumn annals) meant that at the turn of the Qin-Han dynasties, the astrologers' concern was to match the nine prefectures on land with the nine spaces of the sky, not twelve prefectures.

The '*jun-tian*' centric sky with the Horn, Neck and Root mansions of the eastern skies in *Lv-shi Chun-qiu*'s nine '*fen ye*' allocated territories, which was mapped to the Yuzhou prefecture or the Zhou king's land, in the twelve '*fen ye*' allocated territories, was equivalent to i) the state of Haan (Horn, Neck, Root) in *Han Shu*; and ii) the state of Zheng or the Yanzhou prefecture (Horn, Neck, Root) and the state of Soong (Room and Heart) or the Yuzhou prefecture in *Jinn Shu*. Unlike the twelve '*fen ye*' divisions that were based on the ecliptic line and often saw one lunar mansion spreading across two sector divisions of the ecliptic, the nine '*fen ye*' division, building on top of the four astral quarters, possessed a centric block [with the neatly-included Horn, Neck and Root mansions] or 'jun-tian' central high sky, plus eight quarters of the astral skies. In *Shi-ji*, there were several entries about the Soong state's '*fen ye*' being the Heart mansion. In *Han Shu*, the three additional prefectures of Bingzhou, Youzhou, and Yingzhou were purportedly carved out of the Jizhou prefecture. The nine or twelve prefectures would become the administrative blueprint of all the future dynasties starting from the Han dynasty, with the nine or twelve prefectural administrative seats in charge of the dozens of commanderies and counties.

From the angle of appearance of the geographical terms, it could be discerned that *Yu Gong* was written after the Chu people's expansion to the concave-in area of the L-shaped Han-shui River in the 8th-7th centuries B.C., where mount Jing-shan was appropriated, and about the time of the Yue state's demise in the hands of the Chu state --either Yue King Wujiang (Wuqiang)'s death during Zhou King Xianwang's 36th year or 333 B.C. per *The Bamboo Annals* or Chu King Huaiwang's defeating the Yue army in 311 B.C. per *Chu Ce* of *Zhan Guo Ce*. This was because the appearance of the Yangzhou prefecture could very much have something to do with the Yang-yue people, one of the Hundred Yue people of southern China.

Guan Zongchang of Dalian Minzu College pointed out that the nine prefectures' school of thought originated from *Yu Gong*, underwent modification as seen in Zou Yan's Greater Nine Prefectures' theory and Lv Buwei's book *Lv-shi Chun-qiu* (its *You-shi Lan* [having a beginning] chapter), had further developments in *Zhou Li* (Zhou rites), *Yi Zhou Shu* [Zhou Dynasty's extant book] and *Er Ya* (close to the 'Ya' or capital district spoken language), took a dramatic change in *Huai Nan Zi*, and was further expanded on in *He-tu Kuo Di Xiang* (the image encompassing land) and *Shi Zhou Ji* (book on ten continents). Using *Huai Nan Zi* as a division line, Guan Zongchang's point on some dramatic change in the nine prefectures' cosmological view was that the order of the nine prefectures was at first varied and ambiguous [but similar to *Yu Gong*]; however, after *Huai Nan Zi*, the order became serialized, namely, starting from the southeastern direction [where Shenzhou {the divine prefecture} or 'nong-tu' {agricultural land} was] and moving clockwise. Guan Zongchang claimed that the new order of nine prefectures, while not treating Jizhou as the first prefecture as *Yu Gong* did, specifically remarked that it was the center of all prefectures. Namely, a compromise of *Yu Gong* and Zou Yan's nine greater prefectures. Calling the nine prefectures by virtual, illusory and imaginary, Guan Zongchang cited Yang Shuda in stating that the names of the nine prefectures in *Huai Nan Zi* must have come from Zou Yan's nine greater prefectures. Guan Zongchang was correct that the author of *Huai Nan Zi*, with intent to avoid conflicting with the *Yu Gong* order of prefectures, deliberately applied the virtualization effect to its fuzzy list of nine prefectures, with implication that *He-tu* and other astrological prefectures had to come after *Huai Nan Zi*. However, the truth was more likely that Zou Yan never had a list of nine greater named prefectures; that the astrology-related nine prefectures were construed after *Yu Gong*, *Lv-shi Chun* and *Yi Zhou Shu*; and that the initial nine prefectures of *Yu Gong* could be properly termed the epic or poetic prefectures.

The perspective of Sinitic China with the territories of nine prefectures or nine domains was first seen in *Shi-jing* and *Zuo Zhuan*.

Chang Fa (perpetual development) of *Shang1 Song* in *Shi-jing* talked about 'jiu wei', namely, 'jiu you4' (the nine hunting gardens), and 'jiu you3' (nine 'you'-prefixed tribal domains) --with both 'jiu wei' and 'jiu you' taken to be equivalent to the Zhou dynasty terminology of 'jiu zhou' (i.e., nine prefectures). In Lu Lord Xianggong's 4th year of *Zuo Zhuan* or 569 B.C., Lord Yu was eulogized for the division of land into the nine prefectures and the opening-up of nine channels (or paths). *Zuo Zhuan*, in a later section on Lu Lord Zhaogong's 4th year or 538 B.C., specifically pointed to the mountain area to the west of the Xie-yi fief (Nanyang, Henan) as the land of the precarious mountains of the nine prefectures, namely, San-tu (Luhun, Songxian, Henan), Si-yue (mountains west of the Xie-yi fief or Nanyang, Henan), Yangcheng (Dengfeng, Henan), Dashi4 (Yangcheng, Henan), Jingshan (Yunyang, Hubei; or another Jingshan in Fuping, Shenxi), and Zhongnan (Wugong, Shenxi). Years later, in 533 B.C., *Zuo Zhuan*, in calling the barbarians living near the Zhou capital city by the 'Yin [sun shade] Rong' or the 'Jiu-zhou [nine greater prefectures] Rong' barbarians, implied that the barbarians migrated there from the land of the ancient "nine prefectures". The barbarians' ancestors, i.e., the Luhun-rong & Jiang-rong barbarians, were implied by *Zuo Zhuan* to have dwelled near the Qin capital city of Yong (Fengxiang, Shenxi), or in the ancient Yong-zhou prefecture, before the resettlement near the Zhou capital city in 638 B.C.

Fu Sinian, after analysis of the "Xie-xi zhi jiu-zhou" in *Zheng Yu* of *Guo Yu*, concluded that the ancient "nine prefectures" were located in the mountain area to the west of the Xie-yi fief (Nanyang, Henan). By the Warring States time period, Zou Yan (Zou-zi, ? 305-240 B.C.) extrapolated on the 'Jiu-zhou [nine greater prefectures] zhi Rong' term in making a claim that Sinitic China, i.e., the red-county divine prefecture with the nine minor prefectures, was merely one of eighty-one prefectures or one of the nine major prefectures. Possibly in the aftermath of Sinitic China's territorial expansion in the late Warring States' time period, the nine minor prefectures were modified into twelve prefectures, as seen in *Wu-di Ben-ji* of *Shi-ji* and *Yao Dian* of *Shang-shu* or the split *Shun-dian* chapter of *Shang-shu* of the 3rd and 4th centuries A.D.

The cosmological view of the Nine Greater Prefectures under-went the expansion of four polars in *Lv-shi Chun-qiu* in the late Qin times to eight polars (poles; struts; extremity; culmen per David Pankenier) in *Huai Nan Zi* of the Han dynasty, with the eight im-aginary '*ba yin2*' all-lakes wilderness lying beyond the nine pre-fectures, the eight '*ba hong2*' all-land wilderness lying beyond the '*ba yin2*' belt, and the eight '*ba ji*' or eight polars further beyond --that had eight gates acting as valves to control the air flow or clouds. This was built on top of Zou Yan's Greater Nine Prefec-tures' theory which talked about two rings of seas, with a middle ring called the Pi-hai Seas (small seas) and an outer ring called the Da-ying-hai Seas (large seas).

Astrologically, in the late Warring States and the early Han dyn-asty, there was a flurry of nine fable prefectures with varying names, as seen in the Shanghai Museum bamboo slips *Rong-cheng-shi*, in the *Di-xing Xun* (earth's shape and terrain) section of *Huai Nan Zi*, and in *Zhang Heng Zhuan* (biography on Zhang Heng) of *Hou Han Shu*, and in *He-tu Kuo Di Xiang* (map on the back of the dragon from the Yellow River; the image encompassing land) of the *He-tu Wei* prophecy series of the Han dynasty. The main point of the nine fable prefectures was the one-to-one correspondence of the astral sector divisions with the land of the vassal states on earth, with the coverage of i) the heaven's nine orbits (trajectories of the iplanet {i.e., the grand one} and five planets, etc.) [or nine components (i.e., the Big Dipper, the ecliptic, and the Centaurus)] and eight orders (i.e., four seasons, sun, moon, solstice, equinox, etc.) and ii) the earth's nine prefectures and eight pillars. The presence of Liangzhou in *Yu Gong* and the re-placement of Liangzhou by the astral Yongzhou prefecture could shed light on the relative early age of the authorship of *Yu Gong* in comparison with the prevalence of the allocated field ('*fen ye*') in astrology, that corresponded with the heavenly sectors ('*ci*') of the ecliptic –that were measured by the units of degrees ('*ci du*').

While the ancient "nine prefectures" terminology was seen in Lu Lord Xianggong's 4th year of *Zuo Zhuan* or 569 B.C., as well as seen on the bronzeware *Qi-hou Bo Zhong* (marquis Qi's flat-mouth bell) [on which there was a statement about Shang King Shang-tang's receiving the mandate of heaven, i.e., in inheriting the nine prefectures and residing at Lord Yu's capital city], there never existed an enumeration of the names of nine prefectures in the ancient literature like *Zuo Zhuan*. *Zuo Zhuan* merely carried the names of Guazhou which was the 'Jiu-zhou-zhi-rong' barbarians' homeland, the 'Rongzhou' settlement next to Wey Lord Zhuanggong's capital city, Yang2zhou (sunny prefecture) of the Lu state, Pingzhou of the Qi state, and Xiazhou (Xia prefecture –with settlement of the Chen-guo people) of the Chu state.

Furthermore, there was no definite record as to the existence of Lord Yu's nine cauldrons. According to Lu Lord Xuan'gong 3rd year of *Zuo Zhuan*, Lord Yu's cauldrons carried the images of 'bai wu', i.e., hundreds of objects (i.e., sacrificial animals per Kwang-chih Chang, that could connect heaven with earth), from the remote lands, when they were cast with the nine pieces ['jiu mei'] of copper submitted as tributes by the remote lands ['yuan fang'], not the nine prefectures, at a time when the Xia dynasty possessed the virtues. On another occasion, *Zuo Zhuan*, in Lu Lord Zhaogong's 12th year or 530 B.C., talked about an assumption made to the ill-fated Chu King Lingwang from Chu minister Zi-ge, which was an answer to i) the Chu king's question about Zhou King Kangwang's refusal to share the Zhou ritual instruments with Chu ancestor Xiong Yi and ii) the Zheng state's possibility of yielding the [Jiu-]xu land that the Chu's remote ancestor 'huang-zu bofu' Kunwu dwelled. Zi-ge answered: "How could the Zheng state be parsimonious about the old Xu[3]-guo land when the Zhou king would share the cauldrons [--that were not prefixed with nine]?" It could be the later people who speculated that Lord Yu or Yu the Great manufactured nine cauldrons using the nine pieces of copper [from the remote lands --that did not necessarily equate to the eight prefectures that purportedly surrounded the Jizhou prefecture where Lord Yao's capital city was]. This could be the fundamental cause that Qin King Wuwang was killed by one particular cauldron during the heavy weight lifting at the Zhou King's court, with no other cauldrons mentioned, and that at the time of the Zhou dynasty's demise, the nine cauldrons mysteriously disappeared or as the legends claimed, one of the nine cauldrons fell into the Si-shui River while en route of being shipped to the Qin capital city --with the cauldron lost in the Si4-shui River [near Luoyang] being further mixed up with the Soong state's cauldron from the Tai-qiu temple –that purportedly was lost in the Si-shui River [near Pengcheng]. During the Han dynasty, Sima Qian, in the discourse on Han Emperor Wudi's oblation for heaven and earth at mount Taishan, talked about a mythical and personified 'Tai-di' (Mt. Taishan Overlord) possessing one cauldron, the Yellow Thearch possessing three cauldrons and Lord Yu possessing nine cauldrons --all discourse of the post-book-burning forgery nature.

CHAPTER II
THE NINE PREFECTURES

Below will be the paragraph by paragraph paraphrasing and debunking of *Lord Yu's Tributes*. This was built on the work in "The texts of Confucianism, Part I:of the work in *The Shu King, The Religious Portions of the Shih King, The Hsiao King* (The Sacred Books of China 16)", translated by James Legge. Oxford: Clarendon Press, 1879.

Lord Yu divided the land into nine prefectures. Following the course of the hills and mountains and dredging the rivers, Lord Yu let the land of the nine prefectures manifest the properties and qualities for setting the difference of tributes surrendered.

禹别九州，随山浚川，任土作贡。

Lord Yu settled the land. Following the course of the hills and mountains, Lord Yu cut down the trees for setting up markers. Lord Yu selected the highest mountains and largest rivers [in the nine prefectures] and marked them for making sacrifice.

禹敷土，随山刊木，奠高山大川。

Lord Yu's flood control work was validated by the excavated bronzeware *Sui4-gong Xu* from the Western Zhou dynasty, which carried the words "*duo-shan jun-chuan*" that meant "following the course of the hills and mountains and dredging the rivers", and the words '*cha-di she-zheng*' that meant "differentiating the land and stipulating the taxes". The mud that Lord Yu used for controlling the floods was speculated to be the 'xi-tu' self-growing soil that Lord Yu was said by *Di-xing Xun* of *Huai Nan Zi* to have applied in controlling floods, or the 'xi-rang' self-growing soil Gun or Lord Yu's father misapplied in the flood control, for which the high lord ordered the fire guardian god Zhu-rong to have Gun executed per *Hai-nei Jing* of *Shan Han Jing*. *Chang Fa* of *Shi Jing*, however, merely stated that Lord Yu applied [the mud] to the 'Tu-fang' country down on earth, which was alternatively interpreted to be about 'xia-tu' (land on earth) and its four quarters, namely, '{si-}fang'. Both the bronzeware *Sui4-gong Xu* and the poem *Chang-fa* did not carry the terminology of nine prefectures, with the bronzeware talking about 'tian-xia' (land under the heaven) and the poem talking about Shang ancestor Shang-tang's inheriting 'jiu wei' (nine encircled hunting playgrounds), i.e., 'jiu you4' (nine hunting gardens).

With respect to Jizhou:

冀州

> Lord Yu started the dredging work at Hu-kou (kettle neck, namely, the Meng4-men Yellow River floodgate next to the 'Meng-men-jiuhe-zhi-deng' flat land above Jiu-he (nine rivers) in *Mu-tian-zi Zhuan*). Lord Yu took effective flood-control measures at the mountains of Liang-shan and Qi-shan [to the west of the Yellow River Bend --which was termed Xi-he {west river}, with the dragon gate pierced north of the Liang-shan mountain].

> 既载壶口，治梁及岐。

The Jizhou prefecture could have derived from Ji-fang, a fang-suffixed Shang dynasty terminology that meant land or a country, that was taken to be Lord Yao's homeland termed by Da-xia or the Great Xia land. There was the entry about the Great Xia legacy in *Wu-zi Ge* (*Wu-zi Zhi Ge*) or the five sons' poems of *Shang-shu*: "*wei* [only] *pi* [that] *Tao-tang* [Overlord Tao-tang-shi], *you* [there was] *ci* [this] *ji-fang* [the Grand Xia land]". Five Taikang brothers and their mother made five songs on the north riverbank of Luo, which contained a possibly fallacious number. If it was Taikang's four brothers making four songs calling for the return of the elder brother, it should be termed four songs, not five songs. The historical five brothers' songs are most likely later forgeries. In today's *Xia Shu* section of *Shang-shu*, there were only four chapters, including *Yu Gong, Gan Shi4, Wu-zi Zhi Ge* and *Yin4 Zheng*, with *Wu-zi Zhi Ge* and *Yin4 Zheng* taken to be the forged "ancient" version while the other two chapters were taken to be the Han-dynasty contemporary or orally recited original texts.

The name Jizhou could be seen in Qu Yuan's poem *Li Sao* (sorrowful farewell), in which the poet juxtaposed Jizhou with 'si-hai' (four seas), namely, treating Jizhou as more a fairy land. In *Da-huang Bei Jing* of *Shan Hai Jing*, the Yellow Thearch was described to have ordered Ying-long to defeat and execute Chi-you in the open fields of Jizhou. *Yi Zhou Shu* claimed that the Yellow Thearch caught and executed Chi-you in the middle of the Jizhou land, i.e., 'zhong Ji'. The *Gui-cang Yi* divination texts, however, claimed that the Yellow Thearch killed Chi-you at Qingqiu (green hill) which was likely the origin of the Qingzhou prefecture. Here, it could be seen that Jizhou was more a place naming in a divinatory context than a physical locality.

Historians of the two Soong dynasties had imagination in interpreting the section of the lord's centric prefecture in *Yu Gong*. The Soong historians possibly construed up the flood situation by means of reflecting on the 'Mengmen-jiuhe-zhi-deng' flat land above Jiu-he (nine rivers) in *Mu-tian-zi Zhuan* --which implied a reservoir above the flood gate. Zhu Xi (A.D. 1130-1200) of the Soong dynasty believed that before Lord Yu dredged the river, the Yellow River's water was hindered by the rocks at the Meng-men gate, with the water overflowing beyond the Meng-men gate to form an overflowing situation like a modern sense reservoir. That is, part of the Yellow River's water, because of the hindrance of rocks or mountains at Meng-men [and Long-men {dragon gate} between Hejin {on the east side} and Haancheng {on the west side}], overflew upstream along the Wei-shui River and [Northern-]Luo-he River towards the west side of the Eastern Yellow River Bend while another part of the water, coupling with the Fen-shui River's water, possibly overflew towards the upperstream Fen-shui River [to the direction of Tai-yuan]. The two parts of the Yellow River water then joined forces at Hua-yin (i.e., shady side of the Huashan mountain) before turning east for Dizhu (i.e., steadfast rocky pillar in the middle of the river), where Lord Yu pierced the flood gates on two sides of the Dizhu rock [at today's Sanmenxia] to allow the Yellow River water pass along the enlarged openings along the two sides of the Dizhu rock. Lin Zhiqi (A.D. 1112-1176), who also believed that the water flew inversely towards the Qi-shan mountain to the west, took the Meng-men gate to be located upperstream and to the west of Hu-kou (kettle neck), and claimed that Lord Yu, after Meng-men, opened up the Long-men gate to the north of the Liang-shan mountain. Cheng Dachang (A.D. 1123-1195) took the Meng-men-shan mountain as the start of the dragon gate and the Yellow River's confluence area with the Fen-shui river as the dragon gate exit. Xue Jixuan (A.D. 1134-1173) treated the Liang-shan and Qi-shan flood control work to be part of the upperstream work. While the Liang-shan mountain [that was recorded in *Zuo Zhuan* to have collapsed at one time –one of three incidents of mountain collapse in *Chun-qiu*, and clogged the Yellow River] was on the west side of the Yellow River, the Qi-shan mountain was situated inland along the Wei-shui River. Guo Songtao (A.D. 1818-1891) adopted Xue Jixuan and Lin Zhiqi's opinions that this passage was about Lord Yu's work at Hu-kou, Meng-men and Long-kou (dragon gate), as well as the accomplishments of flood control at Qi-shan (i.e., along the Wei-shui River) to the west and the Tai-yuan and Yue-yang area to the east --areas impacted by the Yellow River's inverse flow along the Fen-shui River. (The dragon gate here, between Hejin and Haancheng, was different from the Yi-que [rostrum-like] dragon gate overlooking the Yi-shui River at the Longmen-shan mountain of Luoyang, as seen in *Mo Zi*, *Shui Jing Zhu* and *Han Shu*.)

This section on the Jizhou Prefecture was frequently misinterpreted over the two words of 'Liang' and 'Qi2', with the former mistaken to be today's mount Lvliang-shan on the eastern riverbank and the latter speculated to be some sub-mountain ranges of Lvliangshan. The common interpretation of 'Qi2' as a branch of the Liang-shan mountain was wrong since the 'Qi2' word recurred in the later passages of *Yu Gong* as a major Yongzhou Prefecture mountain where sacrifice was made.

Lord Yu took effective flood-control measures from Taiyuan (i.e., the upperstream Jinn-shui and Fen-shui Rivers[, not the Taiyuan place of the early Zhou dynasty, which was the upperstream Jing-shui and Wei-shui Rivers of Shenxi]) to Yue-yang (i.e., the area south of Mt. Huo-tai-shan or the area south of the Taihang mountain range, and to the east of today's Zhongtiaoshan Mountain).

既修太原，至于岳阳；

Lord Yu being successful with his repair work in the Tan-huai area (i.e., the horizontal Yellow River flow course area near today's Jiaozuo of Henan, i.e., the land of origin of the Zhang-shui River), went on to repair the west-to-east cross-flowing stream of the Zhang-shui River. The soil of this prefecture was whitish and mellow; its contribution of revenues was the highest of the highest class (i.e., the 1st class), with some proportion surrendering the 2nd class revenues; and its fields were the average of the middle class (i.e., the 5th class).

覃怀砥绩，至于衡漳。厥土惟白壤，厥赋惟上上错，厥田惟中中。

The waters of the Heng-shui River [from mount Heng-shan] and the Wey-shui River [in Lingshou] being brought to their proper channels, the land around the great continental land (Da-lu) lake [north of Julu] was made capable of cultivation.

恒、卫既从，大陆既作。

The region 'Yue-yang', namely, the sunnyside of mount Yue, meant for the area south of the legendary Huoshan or Huo-tai-shan peak, where some deity existed. This could be inferred from the *Shi-ji* records related to the demise of the Zhi-shi clan and the rise of the Zhao state, with three heavenly messengers from Marquis Shanyang-hou of Mt. Huo-tai-shan producing the bamboo knots with prophecy that the Zhi-shi clan would be destroyed. This area, in the 3rd century B.C., was called by the land of Nanyang, i.e., the area south of the Taihang mountain range, that in

263 B.C. Qin attacked and took from the Haan state. The name of Tai-yuan, which originally meant for the high plateau at the origin of the Jing-shui River of today's Shenxi, was appropriated to the upper Fen-shui River after the Jinn state's northward expansion against the Qun-di and Wuzhong barbarians.

The Tan-huai area (i.e., the Da-pi-shan area of Hebi and Junxian under the Yongzhou section, a name possibly deriving from the Tui2 and Huai2 land of the Wen-di fief that Zhou King Wuwang assigned to justice minister Su Fensheng, with the 'Huai2' word seen in Lu Lord Yin'gong's 11th year of *Zuo Zhuan*) was taken by *Yuanhe jun-xian tu zhi* (maps and books on the commanderies and counties during the Yuanhe Era), a book written by Li Jifu of the Tang dynasty, to be about the Jizhou prefecture land near the Yellow River. This was probably based on Zheng Xuan's comment that Tanhuai was a county in the He-nei-jun commandery, namely, the Nan-yang land of the Jinn state on the northern riverbank, an area awarded by Zhou King Xiangwang to Jinn Lord Wen'gong. This region, termed Huai-shan and Xiangling in *Yao Dian* of *Shang-shu*, belonged to the Shang dynasty's capital district area..

Both the Yue-yang place and the Tan-huai area are considered part of the Yin-guo fief and later the He-nei-jun territory of the Han dynasty, which was located at the eastern end of the He-dong-jun commandery and the northern end of the San-chuan-jun commandery of the Qin dynasty.

> The Dao-yi barbarian people of the islands, with the dresses of furs and skins, sailed into the Yellow River to surrender the tributes by keeping their ships close to the coastline along the Jie-shi rocks to the right (i.e., using the Jie-shi tablet mountain near today's Mountain and Sea Pass as the beacon tower equivalent).

岛夷皮服，夹右碣石入于河。

Note that the ancient book *Yu Gong* made a difference between the Dao-yi and Niao-yi while the two characters later corrupted into each other to mean the wrong Yi group. The skin-wearing island Yi people in today's southeastern Manchuria were different from the bird totem Yi in the Yangtze River area, who were described to have the 'hui-fu' clothes –that was speculated by Wu Chunming of Xiamen University as the southern barbarians and Pacific islands' tree bark cloth. *Yu Gong* could have been transcribed in different orders of the Dao-yi and Niao-yi barbarians in history.

With respect to Yanzhou:

兖州

Between the Ji-shui River and the Yellow River was the Yanzhou prefecture (i.e., a prefecture name pinpointed by *Lv-shi Chunqiu* to be the land of the former Wey Principality; and a prefecture name that was speculated to have derived from a 'western' Yan3 zhou place from the *He Tu* book {if *He Tu* was as ancient as the Warring States time period} and also cited by Han dynasty book *Huai Nan Zi*, with the closest soundex being the ancient Yan-guo state that Duke Zhou-gong conquered in the early Zhou dynasty]. The Nine [Tributary] Rivers of the Yellow River {in the Hebei plains} being dredged to keep their proper channels, the Lei-xia land was made into a lake, into which the waters of the Yong-shui and the Ju-shui (Qu-shui) flew together. The mulberry-tree grounds being made fit for raising the silkworms, the people came down from the hills to make homes on the grounds below. The soil of this prefecture was blackish and rich; its grass was luxuriant, and the trees grew high. Its fields were the lowest of the middle class (i.e., the 6th class), with its contribution of revenue fixed at what would just be deemed the correct amount, namely, i.e., the 9th class --which would take cultivation for thirteen years before reaching the production level of the other eight prefectures. Its articles of tribute were varnish (lacquer) and silk, and in baskets were surrendered the woven ornamental fabrics. The people of Yanzhou floated along the Ji-shui and Luo4-shui (Ta-shui) Rivers, and so reached the Yellow River [for surrendering tributes to the lord's capital city in Jizhou, i.e., the Great Xia land].

济河惟兖州。九河既道，雷夏既泽，灉、沮会同。桑土既蚕，是降丘宅土。厥土黑坟，厥草惟繇，厥木惟条。厥田惟中下，厥赋贞，作十有三载乃同。厥贡漆丝，厥篚织文。浮于济、漯，达于河。

Yu Gong, in this passage, possibly derived the Yanzhou Prefecture's name on basis of the ancient Yan3-guo state, which was at one time the former Shang dynasty's capital city and later a Shang dynasty stalwart ally that Archduke Zhou-gong defeated. This place was the famed Shao-hao-shi Ruins from antiquity, i.e., what Viscount Tan-zi of the Tan-guo state claimed to be ancestor Shao-hao's country. During the three-year war, Duke Zhou-gong and King Chengwang attacked the Huai-yi (ancient Xu2-guo state) people around the Huai River, and attacked the ex-Shang Marquisdom of Yan3-guo fief (i.e., the Shao-hao-shi Ruins) and relocated the Yan3-guo marquis away from the area of today's Qufu County, Shandong Province.

In *He-tu Kuo Di Xiang* (map on the back of the dragon from the Yellow River; the image encompassing land) of the *He-tu Wei* prophecy series of the Han dynasty, there was reference to a Yann3-zhou prefecture in the straight west direction, namely, one of the nine earthly prefectures corresponding with one of the nine components (i.e., the Big Dipper, the ecliptic, and the Centaurus)] of the heaven.

With respect to Qingzhou:

青州

Between the sea and the Taishan mountain was the Qingzhou prefecture (i.e., a 'green' name that possibly derived from the azure dragon astral quarter). The Yu-yi (corner Yi) barbarians' territory being under control, the Wei-shui [from mount Jiwu-shan of Langya] and Zi-shui [from Laiwu] Rivers were made to keep their channels. Its soil was whitish and rich, and along the seashore were the wide tracts of salty land. Its fields were the lowest of the first class (i.e., the 3rd class), and its contribution of revenue the highest of the second (i.e., the 4th class). Its articles of tribute were salt, the fine cloth of dolichos fiber, productions of the sea of various kinds, silk and hemp from the small valleys of the Taishan mountain, lead, pine trees, and strange stones (i.e., jagged rocks of grotesque shapes). The Lai-yi barbarian people [from mount Lai-shan] being taught the rule by 'mu' (shepherd chancellor, --one of three administrative posts in *Li Zheng* (establishing administration) of *Shang-shu*, i.e., '*chang-bo*' ('*li-shi*'), '*chang-ren*' ('*mu-fu*', '*mu*') and '*zhun-ren*' --that were termed three kinds of evaluation of ministers (i.e., 'san zhai' [three foundation {evaluation}])), surrendered as tributes in their baskets were the silk from the mountain mulberry tree. They floated along the Wen-shui River, and so reached the Ji-shui River [for transfer to the Yellow River for a continuous trip to the Jizhou prefecture].

海岱惟青州。嵎夷既略，潍、淄其道。厥土白坟，海滨广斥。厥田惟上下，厥赋中上。厥贡盐絺，海物惟错。岱畎丝、枲、铅、松、怪石。莱夷作牧。厥筐檿丝。浮于汶，达于济。

The name of Qingzhou prefecture could have derived from the 'green' name that was the azure dragon astral quarter with the eastern azimuth. It could be related to the place Qingqiu (green hill) in the *Gui-cang Yi* divination texts. *Yu Gong*, in this passage, referred to the Yu-yi [sea corner Yi] and Lai-yi [the Laizhou prefecture Yi] in the ancient Qing-zhou prefecture –before continuing the topics on the Huai-yi [the Huai-shui River Yi] in the ancient Xu-zhou prefecture, the Niao-yi [bird totem Yi] in the ancient Yang-zhou prefecture, plus the He-yi in the ancient Liang-zhou prefecture. While Lai-yi specifically referred to the Lai-guo state, Yu-yi could be a philosophical concept. *Yao Dian*, a different chapter of *Shang-shu*, talked about the four corners of Yu-yi (meaning the later 'corner Yi barbarians', a place called 'Tang-gu' or the hot spring valley), Nan-jiao (the southern outskirts, with the 'jiao' word implying the later 'Jiao-zhi' [Cochin-china] for the crossing toes), Mei-gu (i.e., Ming-gu or the darkness/sunset valley), and Shuo-fang (the northern domain, called by 'You-du' or the dark capital city). In the same article *Yao Dian*, there was reference to four places of exile for the evil tribes, namely, Youzhou (i.e., 'You-du'), Mt. Chong-shan, San-wei (i.e., three precarious mountains), and Mt. Yu-shan (i.e., feather mountain). The four places of exile meant for the four corners of the earth in a philosophical sense.

The section on the Dong-yi barbarians in *Hou Han Shu* stated that the Yi people included such subgroups as Quan-yi [doggy Yi], Yu2-yi, Fang-yi, Huang-yi [yellow Yi], Chi-yi [red Yi], Bai-yi [white Yi], Xuan-yi [black Yi], Feng-yi [wind Yi], Zi-yi, and Yang2-yi [sunny Yi], etc., hence incorporating 'Yi' on an inclusive scale. The colors of yellow, white, etc., for the Yi people, could be designation of the clothing of the Yi people. *The Bamboo Annals* included the Huai-yi [the Huai-shui River Yi] and Lan-yi [blue Yi]. *Yu Gong* (Lord Yu's Tributes) of *Shang-shu* appeared to have a different list of the Yi barbarians. It would be most likely that the former two books either copied or expanded on *Yu Gong* than vice versa.

With respect to Xuzhou:

徐州

Surrounded by the sea, the Taishan mountain, and the Huai-shui River was the Xuzhou prefecture. The Huai-shui River and the Yih2-shui [i.e., Ni-shui, from mount Tai-shan] River being regulated, the land of the Meng-shan and Yu-shan was made fit for cultivation. The waters of Da-ye (big wilderness, i.e., Juye-ze Lake) were confined to form a marsh, the tracts of Dong-yuan (eastern plains) were successfully brought under management. The soil of this prefecture was red, clayey, and rich; and its grass and trees grew more and more bushy. Its fields were the second of the highest class (i.e., the 2nd class); and its contribution of revenue was the average of the second (i.e., the 5th class). Its articles of tribute were the five-colored mud [that was used by the lords for making sacrifice at the Tai-she Temple], the big variegated pheasants from the small valleys of mount Yu-shan, the solitary dryandra from the south of mount Yi-shan, and the sound-making stones that exposed themselves along the riverbanks of the Si-shui River. The Huai-yi barbarian tribes brought over the oyster-pearls and the 'ji-yu' carp fish, and their baskets full of black silken fabrics and white raw silk. They floated along the Huai-shui and the Si-shui Rivers, and so reached the Yellow River [for transfer to the Yellow River for a continuous trip to the Jizhou prefecture].

海、岱及淮惟徐州。淮、沂其乂，蒙、羽其艺，大野既猪，东原砥平。厥土赤埴坟，草木渐包。厥田惟上中，厥赋中中。厥贡惟土五色，羽畎夏翟，峄阳孤桐，泗滨浮磬，淮夷蠙珠暨鱼。厥篚玄纤、缟。浮于淮、泗，达于河。

The Xuzhou place in *Yu Gong* most likely meant for the Pengcheng city or today's Xuzhou, which was different from Qi Honorary-prince Mengchang-jun's Xue-di fief, commonly taken to be today's Xuexian/Tengxian of Shandong or the original Xue-guo state land. The Pengcheng city was a capital equivalent 'yi' city of the Soong Principality through the 6th to 4th century B.C. It was taken to be the locality of the legendary Da-peng-shi country from antiquity. The Pengcheng place or the present Xuzhou city was known as the copper mountain in the ancient times, a reason that the Japanese Army coded the 1938 campaign against Xuzhou as the 'Tozan [copper mountain] Campaign'.

Xuzhou could be a name for multiple places in history. The 'zhou' prefix as seen in *Zuo Zhuan* was merely a prefecture unit below the standard of a capital city and the metropolitan 'yi' fiefs. There was Qu1zhou/Shuzhou (Pingshu, Dacheng, Hebei) where Qi Lord Jian'gong was caught by Qi usurper minister Tian Chang in 481 B.C. and later killed and a Xuzhou place that was described by *Shi-ji* to have its north city gate facing the Yan state and the western city gate facing the Zhao state, where the Wei and Qi states' 335-334 B.C Xuzhou meeting possibly took place; and there was the Xuzhou (Tengxian, Shandong) place where Yue King Gou-jian (r. 496-465 B.C.) convened a summit with lords of the Qi, Soong, Jinn and Lu states, etc. The Xuzhou meeting could be tagged a 'Xuzhou' name like backtracking in the history annals and should the name exist at the time of Gou-jian, it could be actually the Qu1zhou/Shuzhou to the north, i.e., a nexus for the lords of Qi, Soong, Jinn and Lu to meet, instead of the Xue-guo state or the legendary Pengcheng place which was a Soong city and necessitated the Xuzhou meeting as the Pengcheng meeting.

The Xuzhou prefecture's name most likely derived from the former Xu-2guo state's name than the Qu1zhou/Shuzhou (Ping-shu, Dacheng, Hebei) place where Qi Lord Jian'gong was caught by Qi usurper minister Tian Chang in 481 B.C. The Xuzhou name that was Qu1zhou/Shuzhou, with the same 'Xu2' word that was equivalent to the 'Shu1' character, was more likely located at the trilateral border area of the Zhao, Yan and Qi states. The Xuzhou place naming could have only appeared in history after the demise of the Xu2-guo state. It was the Wu state which eliminated the Zhongwu-guo and Xu2-guo states in 512 B.C. Yue King Goujian, after defeating the Wu state in 473 B.C., took over the former Beiliang-yi land (Xu1yi2, Jiangsu), crossed the Huai-shui River and had a summit with lords of the Qi, Soong, Jinn and Lu states, etc., at Xuzhou (Tengxian, Shandong) –if the place naming Xuzhou existed after the Wu conquest of the Xu2-guo state. This meant that *Yu Gong* could not have been written earlier than the 6th century B.C.

Specifically, there was an entry in *The Bamboo Annals* that was put under Wei King Huichengwang's 31st year or 340 B.C., that the Xue-di place was renamed to Xuzhou. According to the extracted texts from the original book *The Bamboo Annals*, there was a [Xia-]pi-guo lord, by the title of Count [or Elder Uncle] Pi-bo, who related to the Xue-di place during Wei King Huichengwang (r. 370-319 B.C.)'s 31st year, namely, 340 B.C., with the Xue-di place renamed to Xuzhou. Namely, the Shang-pi Xue-guo state, which was Qi Marquis Cheng-hou Zou Ji's Qian-yi fief per Qian Mu, relocated to the former Xue-guo land (Tengzhou, Shandong) from Xia-pi (Suining, Jiangsu) during Wei King Huichengwang's 31st year or 340 B.C. per *Shi-ji Suo-yin*, a Chu puppet state that could be possibly swallowed up by the Chu state after Chu King Qingxiangwang's 18th year or 281 B.C. per *Chu Shi-jia*. Disputes existed as to the nature of Count Pi-bo who was speculated to be some descendant of the original Ren-surnamed Xue-guo state which was forced into a southern move in the 5th century B.C. However, by the 4th century B.C., the Qi state had detoured around the Lu state, i.e., the eastern side of mount Taishan, to have occupied the place of today's Xuzhou (Tengxian, Shandong). According to *Lv-shi Chunqiu*, the Lu state acquired Xuzhou possibly in the aftermath of Qi King Minwang (r. 300-284 B.C. per Qian Mu & Yang Kuan; wrong reign 323-284 B.C. per *Shi-ji*)'s demise. In 1954, there was excavation of the *Pi-bo Chui* (*Pi-bo Lei*) bronzeware in Yixian of Shandong, namely, the locality of the Xue-guo state, which validated the Pi-guo state's relocation to the Xiapi place in the early Warring States' time period.

The Xue-di Xuzhou in today's southern Shandong was different from the 5th century B.C. Xuzhou which was located in today's northwestern Shandong, nor the legendary Pengcheng city or today's Xuzhou of Jiangsu. The Xuzhou name in *Yu Gong* was apparently a virtualized name that might not pinpoint any of three places that bore the Xuzhou tag. Inferring from the above historical events in regards to Xuzhou, it could be discerned that the first appearance of Xuzhou in 481 B.C. had nothing to do with the Xu2-guo people who were termed by 'zhu-Xia' (various Xia people) and treated as equivalent to the Xu-rong or Xu-yi barbarians. And the second appearance of Xuzhou in 340 B.C. could be an acknowledgment of existence of the locality of the Xue-guo state being located in about the domain of the 'zhu-Xia' (various Xia people), namely, the Xu2-guo state. The book *Yu Gong*, for the adoption of a Xuzhou prefecture in the spirits of the 340 B.C. renaming of the Xue-di place, could be said to be written about the late 4th century B.C., i.e., in the mid-to-late Warring States time period. Or it could be written earlier if the Xue-di Xuzhou had nothing to do with Xuzhou in *Yu Gong*. (Note Joseph Needham believed that *Yu Gong* was a writing of the 5th century B.C. In contrast with Li Xueqin who believes that *Yu Gong* was written at the end of the Western Zhou dynasty, Gu Jiegang, Wei Juxian, Li Taifen, and Zhang Xitang, et al., believed that the book was written in the late Warring States time period. Li Taifen, however, was wrong in mistaking Lao-zi as a real person, with the *Lao Zi* works treated as earlier than Confucius' works *The Analects*. Li Taifen inadvertently inverted the relationship of the two books *Lao Zi* and *Sun-zi Bing Fa*. Zhang Xitang, like the doubt-ancient school scholars, was very wrong in making the claim that *Zuo Zhuan* was forged by Lin Xin of the Han dynasty. Wang Guowei, an erudite, stated in *Gu-shi Xin Zheng* (New Validation of Ancient History) that *Yu Gong* was likely written at the start of the Zhou dynasty)

With respect to Yangzhou:

扬州

Between the Huai-shui River and the sea was the Yangzhou prefecture [--a name that might have mutated from the Yang-yue people, a variety of the Hundred Yue people of southern China]. The Pengli lake being conserved with the water [from the upper-stream rivers], the sun birds (swans) took the reeds as their home. The three Jiang1 rivers being properly diverted [downstream towards the East Sea], the Zhen-ze (Tai-hu) lake was finally settled. The bamboos, small and large, spread about the area; the grass grew thin and long; and the trees rose high. Its soil was miry; and its fields were the lowest of the lowest class (i.e., the 9th class); and its contribution of revenue was the highest of the lowest class (i.e., the 7th class), with a proportion of the class above (i.e., the 8th class). Its articles of tribute were gold, silver, and copper (or three-colored copper per Zheng Xuan (A.D. 127-200)); the 'yao' and 'kun' jades and jade stones, and the bamboos, small and large; and the elephants' trunks, rhino hides, feathers, yak tails, and timber. The Niao-yi [bird pitch accented] barbarian people wore the garments of tree barks, with silks woven in the shell-patterns in their baskets. Their bundles of tributes contained small oranges and pumeloes, rendered when specially required under the lord's 'xi-ming' decree. They followed the course of the Jiang-shui River and the sea coast, and so reached the Huai-shui and the Si-shui Rivers [for transfer to the Yellow River for a continuous trip to the Jizhou prefecture].

淮海惟扬州。彭蠡既猪，阳鸟攸居。三江既入，震泽砥定。筱、簜既敷，厥草惟夭，厥木惟乔。厥土惟涂泥。厥田唯下下，厥赋下上，上错。厥贡惟金三品，瑶、琨、筱、簜、齿、革、羽、毛惟木。鸟夷卉服。厥篚织贝，厥包橘柚，锡贡。沿于江、海，达于淮、泗。

The two characters of Yang2 and Yang [in Yangzhou of *Yu Gong*] were different, with the Yang2zhou places on the Shandong peninsula related to the ancient Yang2-yi [sunny Yi], i.e., one of the famed Nine Eastern Yi people. Among the astrology-related nine prefectures, Yang2zhou prefecture [sunny prefecture] was seen in *Huai Nan Zi* and *Chu Xue Ji*, two books that might have copied the nine prefectures' soundex names from *He Tu*. There were several Yang2zhou places in *Zuo Zhuan* and *Chun Qiu*, that were located on the Shandong peninsula. In the 2nd year of Lu Lord Min'gong or 660 B.C., *Chun Qiu* recorded that the Qi state uprooted the Yang2-guo (sunny) state, i.e., the expulsion of the Yang2-guo people to purportedly today's Yih-shui River area from today's Yexian (armpit county) on the eastern Shandong peninsula. The Yang2-guo people, like the Ju3-guo state, could be the sun-worshipping natives of the peninsula. There existed a Ju3-guo ancestral reverence monument at the Wangxianjian (fairy seeking) Creek of Rizhao County, that was looted in 1899by the German army in the aftermath of the "Clergymen Incident of Rizhao (sunshine shower) County". *Zuo Zhuan*, at least on two occasions, mentioned Yang2zhou. In 542 B.C., Qi minister Zi-wei, who schemed to kill minister Lvqiu Ying, ordered Lvqiu Ying to attack Yang2zhou (sunny prefecture, i.e., Dongping, Tai'an, Shandong) of the Lu Principality; and in January of 502 B.C., Lu Lord Dinggong invaded the Qi state and attacked Yangzhou. However, the name Yangzhou, which designated the territory southeast of the Chu, Lu and Qi states, had to have origin from the Yang-yue people, a variety of the Hundred Yue people of southern China. The Yang-yue name was seen in *Chu Shi-jia* section of *Shi-ji*, wherein Chu ancestor-king Xiong Qu was said to have expanded in the Jiang1-Han River area, namely, the Han-shui River, attacked the Yong1 and Yang-yue states.

In this passage, the three Jiang1 rivers were widely debated on in history, with historians either pointing to the upperstream Yangtze or lowerstream Yangtze for three rivers. Syntactically speaking, the three Jiang1 rivers should be located within the Yangzhou prefecture, not beyond that. Hence, the three Jiang1 rivers might not have anything to do with the ambiguous Jiang1-shui River [i.e., 'zhong-jiang' or the Middle River from Mt. Min-shan], the Han-shui River [i.e., the 'bei-jiang' or the Northern River from Bozhong-shan], and the unidentified river [that was speculated to be the Gan-jiang River by Soong dynasty historian Su Shi]. And, the three Jiang1 rivers, of course, had no relationship with the three rivers in *Shan Hai Jing*. Namely, Mt. Min-shan's three rivers in the *Hai-nei Dong Jing* section, with 'da-jiang' or the big river coming out of Mt. Wen-shan, 'bei-jiang' or the northern river coming out of Mt. Man-shan, and 'nan-jiang' or the southern river coming out of Mt. Gao-shan. Note that *Yu Gong* made a difference between the Dao-yi and Niao-yi while the two characters later corrupted into each other to mean the wrong Yi group. The skin-wearing island Yi people in today's southeastern Manchuria were different from the bird totem Yi in the Yangtze River area, who were described to have the 'hui-fu' clothes –that was speculated by Wu Chunming of Xiamen University as the southern barbarians and Pacific islands' tree bark cloth (or the grass-knit cloth per the conventional interpretation).

With respect to Jingzhou:

荆州

Between the Jing-shan mountain and the south of mount Heng2-shan was the Jingzhou prefecture. The Jiang-shui and the Han-shui Rivers pursued their course towards the sea as if hurrying to the [spring season] pilgrimage court meeting [with the son of heaven]. The nine rivers (Jiu-jiang) being brought into the status of a full body of water [or the Jiang1-shui River being channeled into nine streams in the middle of the land per Kong Yingda (A.D. 574-648)], the Tuo-shui (Te-shui) and Qian-shui Rivers were put under the constraint of their proper channels. The marsh land of Yun and Meng [at the south and north ends of the marshland] was made capable of cultivation. The soil of this prefecture was miry; its fields were the average of the middle class (i.e., the 8th class); and its contribution of revenue was the lowest of the highest class (i.e., the 3rd class). Its articles of tribute were the feathers, yaks' tail, the elephants' trunks, and rhino hides; and the three metals of gold, silver, and copper (or three-colored copper per Zheng Xuan (A.D. 127-200)). Plus the chun trees, the gan4 trees (wood for making bows), gua1 trees (cedars), and cypresses; and grindstones, whetstones, flint stones (to make the arrow heads), and the cinnabar. [Out of all wood,] only the long bamboos of jun1, the long thorns of lu4, and the hu4 tree, [all good for making arrows], the [three kinds of] famed tributes were the three vassalage states' best specimens. Plus the 'jing-mao' [tulip-scent] thatch grass [for making wines aromatic and precipitating sediments] being sent in with the wrapped bundles and put into cases; the baskets filled with silken fabrics, reddish black and light red, and the strings of pearls; and the great tortoise from the Nine Rivers area at the lord's special 'xi-ming' decree for surrender of tributes. The tributes floated down the Jiang1-shui, the Tuo-shui, the Qian-shui, and the Han-shui Rivers, and hopped across the land to the Luo-shui River, whence they reached the 'nan-he' (south river, i.e., the west-to-east Bend from Huayin to Mengjin to Luo-rui) of the Yellow River.

荆及衡阳惟荆州。江、汉朝宗于海，九江孔殷，沱、潜既道，云土、梦作乂。厥土惟涂泥，厥田惟下中，厥赋上下。厥贡羽、毛、齿、革惟金三品，杶、干、栝、柏，砺、砥、砮、丹，惟菌、簵、楛；三邦砥贡厥名。包匦菁茅，厥篚玄纁玑组，九江纳锡大龟。浮于江、沱、潜、汉，逾于洛，至于南河。

The passage on the Jingzhou prefecture probably revealed the possible origin of the author of *Yu Gong* as a Chu Principality person. Should this claim be said to be reckless, then historian Bao Shouyi's pointing to Xi-he (i.e., the West Yellow River) and Nan-he (i.e., South Yellow River) as evidence that the author of *Yu Gong* was a Chu Principality person was even more reckless. (Here, Nan-he was part of the land of 'san-he' [three river domains], namely, the He-bei [north-of-the-Yellow-River Shang capital district] territory, the He-nan [south-of-of-the-Yellow-River non-Zhou] territory, and the He-rui [Yellow-River-inflection] territory. This 'Nan-he' was different from the segment of the Yellow River in *Mu-tian-zi Zhuan*, that was near the piled-up rocks at the Northeastern Yellow River.)

From the angle of appearance of the Jingshan geographical term, it could be discerned that *Yu Gong* was written after the Chu people's expansion to the concave-in area of the L-shaped Han-shui River in the 8th-7th centuries B.C., where mount Jing-shan was appropriated. Namely, *Yu Gong* could not be a Xia dynasty works, nor a Shang dynasty works. *Zuo Zhuan* stated that the Chu state used the Fangcheng-shan mountain as the city wall against Qi Lord Huan'gong's 656 B.C. military parade towards Jingshan, the gateway to the Chu's Fangcheng city. The Jingshan mountain here was today's Fangcheng, between Nanyang and Xuchang, not the Jingshan mountain Jingshan (Yunyang, Hubei) to the southwest of the L-shaped Han-shui River, nor the [north-of-the-Qinling] Jin-gshan mountain in today's Fuping of Shenxi.)

This passage contained the geographical term 'Jiu-jiang' (nine rivers) that was very much abused by the later historians. Under the "river diversion" heading of *Yu Gong*, Mt. Min-shan was taken to be where the Jiang1-shui River's origin was, with its water flowing east to be the Tuo2 River --which flowed east to the Li3 place where it crossed the "nine rivers" area to become the 'zhong-jiang' or the Middle River. Zhou King Muwang was noted in *The Bamboo Annals* to have raised nine armies to attack east, reaching as far as Jiu-jiang (nine rivers), with turtles and tortoises caught to make a bridge. *Yu Gong* described Jiu-jiang to be full of the overflowing water in the context of i) the Tuo2 River and Qian2 River being the source of water and ii) Lake Yun-Meng [cloudy dreams, or the two lake side areas called by cloud and dream – possibly related to the Yunzhong-jun {in the clouds} god] being a buffer zone, with big turtles and tortoises seen in the "nine rivers" area.

This was a statement similar to the *Zhi-fang* [tribute domain] section in *Xia Guan* [Xia dynasty ministers] of the later book *Zhou Guan* [Zhou dynasty ministers]. (In the Han dynasty, Lord Yu was said by Han Emperor Wudi to have dredged 'jiu-jiang' (nine [minor] rivers) and 'si-du' (four lakes/major rivers), with 'Jiu-jiang' apparently being treated as a nationwide system of rivers.)

Here, 'Jiu-jiang' (nine rivers) apparently meant for the marshland at the Han-shui River inflection area before the concept was appropriated southward or southeastward towards the Huai-shui River of today's Anhui Province where the Qin empire launched the Jiujiang-jun commandery and later the Han dynasty subdivided it into two to three units, with the Jiujiang-jun commandery further appropriated to the Yangtze River area. In the middle mountain range section of *Shan Hai Jing*, Jiu-jiang was defined to be related to the 12th mountain range, which was a northwest-to-southeast running mountain range, with the northwestern baseline at Mt. Jingshan. *Zhong Shan Jing* of *Shan Hai Jing* stated that the high lord's two daughters, who dwelled on Mt. Dongting-shan, swam in the 'Jiang' or Han-shui River's deep-water ponds; and that the winds from the 'Li' and 'Yuan' Rivers crossed the currents above the Xiao-Xiang Rivers' deep-water ponds, with this area called 'Jiu-jiang' or the "nine rivers". From *Yu Gong*, it could be ascertained that the Jiu-jiang [nine rivers] area and the Yun-meng [cloudy dreams] lake could be interchangeable, which meant that the area around the Han-shui River inflection area, thousands of years, was indeed the marshland with numerous watercourses, and the character 'nine' could be a virtual number to mean many, not a real number. The Yun-meng [cloudy dreams] lake, known as the Meng-ze lake in *Zuo Zhuan*, was later interpreted to be two regions of 'Yun' (cloud) and 'Meng' (dream) at the south and north ends of the marshland.

With respect to Yuzhou:

豫州

Between the Jing-shan mountain and the Yellow River was the

Yuzhou prefecture. The Yi-shui [from mount Luhun-shan], the Luo-shui [from mount Zhongling-shan], the Chan-shui [from mount Gucheng-shan], and the Jian-shui [from mount Mianchi-shan] Rivers being conducted to the Yellow River, the marsh and riverbank land of Xing (i.e., Xingbo being equivalent to Xing-bei per Guo Songtao) was   conserved into a lake. The waters of the He-ze [Ge-ze per Kong Yingda] lake [in Huling] being channeled, the marsh lake of Meng-zhu was confined by a dyke. The soil of this prefecture was mellow, with the lowland parts being rich, and dark and hard. Its fields were the highest of the middle class (i.e., the 4th class); and its contribution of revenue was the average of the highest class (i.e., the 2nd class), with a proportion of the very highest (i.e., the 1st class). Its articles of tribute were varnish (lacquer), hemp, fine cloth of dolichos fiber, and the boehmerea; the baskets were full of chequered silks, and of fine floss silk; and the stones for making the sounding-stones instruments and the jade stones were rendered when decreed under the lord's 'xi-ming' mandate. They floated along the Luo-shui River, and so reached the Yellow River.

荆河惟豫州。伊、洛、瀍、涧既入于河，荥波既猪。导菏泽，被孟猪。厥土惟壤，下土坟垆。厥田惟中上，厥赋错上中。厥贡漆、枲，絺、紵，厥篚纤、纩，锡贡磬错。浮于洛，达于河。

The name Yuzhou was purportedly derived from the fact that ancient China, per Zhu Kezhen, used to possess elephants in today's central plains area that was today's Henan Province with the abbreviated name of 'Yu'. *Lu-shi Chun-qiu*, a sophistry book, claimed that the Shang tribe had tamed elephants and used them as weapon against the Eastern Yi people. Lord Shun's brother, by the name of 'xiang' (elephant), mutated into a story about Lord Shun's subduing the elephants in the sophistry-nature Confucian book *Mencius*. The elephant taming was taken to be a profession of the Eastern Yi barbarians, i.e., the cause that Mencius called Lord Shun a 'Dong-yi'. The linkage of elephant to Yuzhou, or to Lord Shun's brother, could be merely fables. (Later books, like

Zhou Li and *Er Ya*, bought in with the concept of Yuzhou as the Sinitic land of origin as the You-Xia-zhi-ju habitat and further selected mount Huashan as the bearing-down mountain which was similar to *Zhi-fang Jie*'s paraphrasing. Zhang Yufa, in expounding the equivalency of the ancient You-shen (You-xin) people to the Sinitic 'Hua' (flowery) people, believed that the ancient people treated the tall Song-gao or Songshan mountain as the 'Hua' mountain, namely, the Huashan or Taihua mountain of Yuzhou was not the same as the Huayin mountain at the Yellow River inflection area.)

Yuzhou could actually mean Lord Yu's "great prefecture" or No. 1 prefecture, i.e., "You-Xia-zhi-ju" and the old Xia land, with the No. 1 position possibly concocted as a juxtaposition with Lord Yao's Jizhou prefecture, i.e., the centric prefecture or the Great [new] Xia land. The 'Yu' word meaning No. 1 was in fact corroborated by the book *Lv-shi Chun-qiu* which treated Yuzhou as the first of nine prefectures. The *You-shi Lan* (having a beginning) of *Lv-shi Chun-qiu*, which treated Yuzhou as the first prefecture, corroborated this viewpoint. In divination, 'Yu' was the 16th hexagram in *Zhou Yi*, which had the 'zhen' trigram at the top and the 'kun' trigram at the bottom, while the character 'xiang' (i.e., elephant) denoted image or shape (i.e., 'yao xiang [image]') of the eight trigrams of *Zhou Yi*. The 'gua-ci' dictum of the 'Yu' hexagram claimed that 'Yu' meant extremely big; the 'tuan' dictum of the 'Yu' hexagram claimed that 'Yu' meant action; the 'xiang' dictum of the 'Yu' hexagram claimed that 'Yu' meant thunder; and the 'yao-ci' line dictum of the 'Yu' hexagram, as far as the only nine-four male line was concerned, claimed that this line was the master of the hexagram since all the female lines were subordinate to the male line. (Lu Deming of the Tang dynasty claimed that Zhou King Wenwang designed the 'gua-ci' hexagram dictum; Duke Zhou-gong designed the 'yao-ci' line dictum; and Confucius designed the ten wings. *Shi1 Fa* (the stalk divination rules), albeit using the same eight trigram images and using the same *Shuo Gua* texts of *Zhou Yi*, had different quasi-hexagram names, no 'gua ci' dictums, and no 'yao ci' line statements. Instead, *Shi1 Fa* used the 'yao [line] xiang [image]' for designating heaven, sun, nobleman (i.e., distinguished persons), war, blood, earth, circle, etc. It was speculated the excavated *Shi1 Fa* divination had inherited the original and primitive way of augury.)

With respect to Liangzhou:

梁州

Between south of mount Hua-shan and the Blackwater River was the Liangzhou prefecture. The hills of the Min-shan and Bo[zhong]-shan mountains being capable of cultivation, the Tuo-shui and Qian-shui Rivers were conducted by their proper channels. The hillside roads between the Cai-shan and Meng-shen mountains being paved and leveled [per Wang Yinzhi (1766-1834) or the conventional interpretation of the 'lv' word as making sacrifice to the mountains], the He-yi barbarian tribes' land was successfully operated on. The soil of this prefecture was loose and dark; its fields were the highest of the lowest class (i.e., the 7th class); and its contribution of revenue was the average of the lowest class (i.e., the 8th class), with proportions of the rates immediately above and below. Its articles of tribute were the best quality jades, the metals of iron, silver, steel, and flint stones to make arrow-heads and sounding-making stones. Plus the skins of bears, brown bears (dom gyamuk), foxes, and jackals. The nation of Zhipi [per Zheng Xuan (A.D. 127-200), i.e., a tribe with the woven products of the animals' hair and fur] came from the mountain of Xi-qing (west inclining). They sailed along the course of the Huan-shui River (possibly the Bai-long-jiang {white dragon} River); then floated along the Qian-shui River, then hopped across the land to the Mian-shui River; then entered the Wei-shui River; and entered and ferried across [the strong currents of] the Yellow River [to the north riverbank where the lord's capital city was].

华阳、黑水惟梁州。岷、嶓既艺，沱、潜既道。蔡、蒙旅平，和夷砥绩。厥土青黎，厥田惟下上，厥赋下中，三错。厥贡璆、铁、银、镂、砮磬、熊、黑、狐、狸、织皮，西倾因桓是来，浮于潜，逾于沔，入于渭，乱于河。

The prefecture name Liangzhou could have derived from the Liangshan mountain. There were two Liangshan mountains, with Count Liang-bo's Liangshan Mountain being possibly a mountain overlooking the Yellow River. The Liangshan Mountain in *Yu Gong* was likely in today's Qianxian County, Xian'yang City, Shenxi, which bordered with the Qi-shui River and Fufeng/Linyou to the west. Gu-gong-danfu, being attacked by the Rong & Di and Xun-yu barbarians, relocated to Mount Qishan, where the bachelor was married with a Jiang-surnamed woman, i.e., 'Jiang nv' in *Shi[-jing]*, hence [re-]starting the Ji-Jiang intermarriage for the next thousand years. Gu-gong-danfu crossed Mt. Liangshan in the southern relocation to Mt. Qishan. Note that the Qin people or the Zhou people's land was classified under the Yongzhou prefecture rather than the Liangzhou prefecture in accordance with the twelve sector divisions of the ecliptic, which could validate the age of the book *Yu Gong* to be earlier than the astrological concepts of the twelve sector divisions of the late Warring States time period.

Yu Gong, in this passage, mentioned a group of the barbarian people called by Zhipi [per Zheng Xuan (A.D. 127-200), i.e., a tribe with the woven products of the animals' hair and fur], that was repeated in the Yongzhou prefecture. This could be the Yuan-rong (Huan2-rong) barbarians, who carried the name of an ancient river called by Yuan-shui (Huan2-shui) and were noted as the He-yi barbarians in *Yu Gong*, near the legendary Mt. Bozhong-shan and the bird-rat-same-cave [i.e., bat cave] mountain. They travelled along the Huan-shui River {*Xiqing ying Huan er lai*}, then floated on the Qian-shui River {*fu yu Qian*}, then cross-hopped into the Mian-shui River {*yu yu Mian*}, then entered and ferried across the Wei-shui River {*ru yu Wei*}, and finally sailed in the Yellow River {*luan yu He*} for Lord Yao/Lord Yu or the Xia dynasty's capital city which was apparently located north of the Yellow River line. In the second mountain range of *Xi Shan Jing* (western mountain range), there was the repeated *Yu Gong* geographical information about the Han-shui River's origin from Mt. Bozhong-zhi-shan and the Wei-shui River's origin from Niaoshu-tongxue-zhi-shan (bird and rat same cave mountain), while the *Zhong Shan Jing* section of *Shan Hai Jing* repeated *Yu Gong*'s geographical information about the Jiang1-shui River's origin from Mt. Min-shan. The Jiang1-shui River, carrying the same character that later denoted the Yangtze but meaning a totally different rivercourse, apparently flowed in parallel with the Han-shui River in the eyes of ancient Chinese. (During Han Emperor Wudi's time, Zhang Tang explored the possibility of linking up the Mian-shui and Wei-shui Rivers, with his son Zhang Mao failing to utilize the shipping due to the water rapids and reefs. The proposed linkage was to enter the Bao-shui River from the Mian-shui River, and after an overland hop, the shipping continued in the Xie-shui River and the Wei-shui River.)

With respect to Yongzhou:

雍州

Between the Blackwater River and the West River (i.e., the Yellow River Bend separating Shenxi from Shanxi) was the Yongzhou prefecture. The Weak-water (i.e., the Ruo-shui water that could not float a feather) River being channeled westwards, the Jing-shui River was led to mingle its waters with those of the Wei-shui River at the winding area [before moving towards the estuary at the Yellow River]. The Qi-shui and the Ju1-shui Rivers being next conducted in their proper channels [into the {Northern-}Luo-shui River], and the waters of the Feng-shui River found the same receptacle [in moving north to enter the Wei-shui River]. The mountains of Jing-shan and Qi-shan being sacrificed to ['lv-ji', or 'chen-ji' per Kong Yingda, namely, being erected the wood landmarks and launched a mountain road path as part of the sacrifice activities], the Zhongnan-shan and Dun-wu mountains were also regulated, with the repair work all the way to mount Niaoshu-tongxue-zhi-shan (bird and rat same cave mountain). Successful measures being taken with the plains on the high plateaus and the lowland swamps, the flood control work extended to the marsh of Zhu-ye. The country of

San-wei being made habitable, and the San-miao barbarians' affairs were greatly arranged. The soil of the prefecture was yellow and mellow; its fields were the highest of the highest class (i.e., the 1st class); and its contribution of revenue the lowest of the second (i.e., the 6th class). Its articles of tribute were the 'qiu2' jades and the 'lin2' jade stones, and the 'lang2-gan1' [pearl-like] gemstones. Floating past Ji-shi (i.e., the piled-up rocks at today's northeastern Yellow River bend), they sailed on to Long-men (dragon gate) and the West River (i.e., the segment of the Yellow River Bend prior to the inflexion), converging [with the other tribute-bearer delegations] north of the Wei-shui River [prior to the ferry across the main Yellow River course to the north riverbank]. The people of 'Zhipi' (per Zheng Xuan (A.D. 127-200), i.e., the people with the woven products of the animals' hair and fur), Kun-lun, plus the land of Xi-zhi and Ju-sou [--not the conventional interpretation of the people of 'Zhipi' dwelling inside the mountains of Kun-lun, Xi-zhi and Ju-sou mountains], the Western Rong barbarian tribes all submitted to the order of rule.

黑水、西河惟雍州。弱水既西，泾属渭汭，漆沮既从，沣水攸同。荆、岐既旅，终南、敦物，至于鸟鼠。原隰砥绩，至于猪野。三危既宅，三苗丕叙。厥土惟黄壤，厥田惟上上，厥赋中下。厥贡惟球、琳、琅玕。浮于积石，至于龙门、西河，会于渭汭。织皮崐崘、析支、渠搜，西戎即叙。

The name 'Yong' in Yongzhou had an uncertain origin. However, the presence of Liangzhou in *Yu Gong* and the replacement of Liangzhou by the astral Yongzhou prefecture could actually shed light on the relative early age of the authorship of *Yu Gong* in comparison with the prevalence of the allocated field (*'fen ye'*) in astrology. The earliest usage of the 'Yong' word, semantically interpreted to be the Guan-zhong land surrounded by high mountains on four sides, would be the Pi-yong Lake that Zhou King Wenwang used as an academy, which was after the Zhou people's conquest of the 'Yong' place, which was located south of the Wei-shui River. In history, in this wider area where the Zhou people built the capital cities after moving off from Zhouyuan and mount Qishan, there existed several Ji2-surnamed states, such as

i) [Qi{shan}-]yong1, ii) Yong1[-zhou] in today's Fuxian of Shenxi, and iii) Feng[-hao] in today's Xi'an of Shenxi. Feng, like the Mixu state and the Yong1 state, was Ji2-surnamed, i.e., one of the few states carrying one of the archaic name of one of the Yellow Thearch's sons. The later Qin people constructed a Yong[cheng] fort in today's Fengxiang as a capital city for about three hundred years.

In *Yu Gong*, there was a list of the Yongzhou prefecture states or tribes of Zhipi, Kunlun, Xizhi, and Qu2-sou1 as comprising of the Xi-rong or Western Rong barbarians, with Kong Yingda citing Zheng Xuan (A.D. 127-200) to state that Zhipi meant for the people who wore the leather and the other three names were for people living in the three wild mountains of Kunlun, Xizhi, and Qu2-sou1. That is, the name Yongzhou was related to the barbarians, with the Wei-shui River treated as the demarcation line of the ancient Yongzhou prefecture. The boundary of Yongzhou with Sinitic China was at 'Wei-bin' in *Guo Yu*, a book later than *Zuo Zhuan*, namely, the Wei-shui River riverbank. In the Han dynasty, Emperor Liu Bang rezoned the Yongzhou prefecture into over eighty counties under the commanderies of He-shang (above the Yellow River), Wei-nan (south of the Wei-shui River), Zhong-di (central land), Long-xi (west of Longshan) and Shang-jun (upper commandery), having apparently adopted the astrological division of the land under the heaven in accordance with the twelve astral sector divisions of the ecliptic. The Qin people or the Zhou people's land, which should be classified under the Liangzhou prefecture in *Yu Gong*, was astrologically put under the Yongzhou prefecture. In *Tian-wen Zhi* (astronomy) of *Jinn Shu*, the twelve [astrological] prefectures were: Yanzhou, Yuzhou, Youzhou, Yangzhou, Qingzhou, Bingzhou, Xuzhou, Jizhou, Yizhou, Yongzhou, Sanhe (three rivers' area), and Jingzhou. (The land of 'san-he' [three river domains], the Chu Principality's Jingzhou land and the Zhou people's Yongzhou prefecture were covered by the southern vermilion bird quarter of the heaven. The Zhou people's ancestral land was called by 'chun shou' or the quail head.)

In the ancient classics *Zuo Zhuan*, there was a barbarian Guazhou ('gua' [melon]) subprefecture which could be part of the ancient Yongzhou prefecture –should there exist such a name. On one occasion in Lu Lord Zhaogong's 9ᵗʰ year of *Zuo Zhuan*, Zhou King Jing3wang claimed that the Guazhou prefecture was where the barbarians' ancestor Tao-wu was exiled by the ancient [Sinitic] king for guarding against the monsters in the [remote] mountains, namely, the Yun-surnamed cunning barbarians [who were induced to live next to into the Zhou capital city's outskirts area] were descendants of Tao-wu. The Zhou king was referring to Jinn Lord Huigong (650-637 B.C.)'s liaison with the barbarians near the Shaoliang area [of the ancient Yong-zhou prefecture], next to the Qin state. *Zuo Zhuan*, however, did not mention Yongzhou but Guazhou. In Lu

Lord Chenggong's 13ᵗʰ year of *Zuo Zhuan*, Jinn emissary Lv-xiang claimed that the Qin lord and the Bai-di barbarians were located in the same prefecture but did not specify a name of the prefecture. This could be construed as a generic '*zhou*' word meaning domain, not an administrative unit like a prefecture. *Shi-ji*, however, specifically adopted the Yongzhou prefecture as the Qin state's isolated position in the barbarian Yongzhou prefecture [in relative separation from Sinitic China]. Sima Qian could have possibly misinterpreted Qin Lord Xiaogong's words of recalling ancestor Qin Lord Mugong (r. 659-621 B.C.)'s feats of pacifying the Jinn state while nurturing virtues and developing the military might in the area between Qi and Yong ('*Qi-Yong zhi jian, xiu-de xing-wu*'), namely, the Qin state and Qin Lord Mu'gong's occupying the space between mount Qishan and the Yong[cheng] city. The Yongcheng city (Fengxiang, Shenxi), located to the northwest of the Yong-shui River and to the north of the Wei-shui River, served as a Qin capital city from Qin Lord Degong (r. 677-676 B.C.) to Qin Lord Xian'gong (r. 384-361 B.C.). (In Sima Qian's *Shi-ji*, Jia Yi's *Guo-qin Lun*, and later dynasties' writing, the reference to Yong-zhou as the Qin state's homeland was manifest for the prevalent adoption of the astrologically-mapped Yongzhou prefecture. For another example, among Qi Lord Huan'gong's ministers of the 7ᵗʰ century B.C., there was a minister called Yi-ya, possibly a Di barbarian from the ancient Yong-zhou prefecture, for which he was also called by Di-ya by *Dai-dai Li-ji* and *Lun Heng* or Yong-wu (Yongzhou sorcerer) in *Shi-ji Ji-jie.*)

CHAPTER III
THE MENDING WORK
ON THE MOUNTAINS

In the repair work on the mountains, the main mountains were arranged into the ranges extending from west to east, with the later people summarizing and tallying the selective mountains of Qianshan, Hukou-shan, Dizhu-shan, Taihang-shan, Xiqing-shan, Xiong'er-shan, Bozhong-shan, Neifang-shan and Wens-han as the famed nine mountains.

Lord Yu surveyed and repaired [the roads and rivers of] the Qian-shan and Qi-shan mountains, proceeding to mount Jing-shan, and then reaching and crossing the Yellow River [after finishing up the flood control work in the concave-out area of the Yellow River inflexion]. From Hu-kou (kettle neck) and the Lei-shou-shan mountain [inside of the concave-in area of the Yellow River inflexion], Lord Yu continued on [with the flood control work to the east of the Yellow River Bend] to the Tai-yue-shan mountain. [After the above flood control work] came the [chiseling operation at] Di-zhu (i.e., the steadfast rock in the midstream of the Yellow River), followed by the repair work at the Xi-cheng-shan mountain (southwest of Huoze/Yangcheng; south of the Wangwu-shan mountain), after he finished work at the Wang-wu-shan (king's house) mountain (northeast of Yuanx-ian, Henan). [Then there was the repair work at the east side of] the Tai-hang-shan and Heng-shan mountains, from which he proceeded to the rocks of Jie-shi (tablet mountain), where the water entered the [Bo-hai] sea.

导岍及岐，至于荆山，逾于河；壶口、雷首至于太岳；砥柱、析城至于王屋；太行、恒山至于碣石，入于海。

Lord Yu conducted work though from the Xi-qing-shan mountain [southwest of Lintao] to Zhu-yu (east of Niaoshu-tongxue-zhi-shan) [to the east], and to Niaoshu-tongxue-zhi-shan (bird and rat same cave mountain) [to the east] and ending in the Tai-hua-shan mountain. Then from the Xiong-er-shan (bear ear) and Wai-fang-shan (outer domain, i.e., mount Songshan in Dengfeng) mountains, Lord Yu conducted work through the Tong-bai-shan mountain range, from which he proceeded to Pei-wei (i.e., Fu-wei, speculated to be mount Queshan which was a small mountain located to the northeast of the tail of the Tong-bai-shan mountain which was the separator of the Han-shui and Huai-shui rivers).

西倾、朱圉、鸟鼠至于太华；熊耳、外方、桐柏至于陪尾。

Lord Yu surveyed and conducted work at the Bo-zhong-shan mountain, going on to the Jing-shan mountain. Then from the Nei-fang (inner domain) mountain, Lord Yu proceeded to the Da-bie-shan mountain.

导嶓冢，至于荆山；内方，至于大别。

From the south of mount Min-shan, Lord Yu went on to mount Heng2-shan (speculated to be near today's Xiong'er-shan, not the mountain between the Huai-shui River and the Yangtze River). Then crossing the Jiu-jiang (nine rivers) marshland area (i.e., the Yun-meng area to the east of the L-shaped Han-shui River area and near today's Suizhou of Hubei), Lord Yu proceeded to the shallow plains of Fu-qian-yuan (Boyangshan/Fuyangshan in Liling of Yuzhang per Yan Shigu).

岷山之阳，至于衡山，过九江，至于敷浅原。

CHAPTER IIV
THE CHANNELING
OF THE RIVERS

In the section on the channeling of the rivers, the exact nine major rivers' systems were detailed as to their repair, diversion and channeling work, starting with the source, continuing with the rivers' flow and confluence with the other rivers, swamps and lakes along their paths, and ending with a statement of their estuaries into the seas. The nine rivers were: Ruo-shui (weak water), Hei-shui (black water), He-shui (Yellow River), Yang-shui, Jiang1-shui, Yan3-shui, Huai-shui, Wei-shui and Luo-shui.

Lord Yu traced the Ruo-shui (weak water) River, with the water channeled as far as the He-li mountain [in Jiuquan], from which its superfluous waters and ripples disappeared into the moving (quick) sands of the Kumtag (or the Liusha[-ze] lake) [west of Dunhuang].

导弱水，至于合黎，馀波入于流沙。

Lord Yu traced the Black-water River [that originated from mount Jishan in Zhangye], with the water channeled [past Dunhuang] as far as the San-wei-shan mountain, from which the water entered the Nan-hai (southern sea) Lake, namely, today's Qinghaihu Lake.

导黑水，至于三危，入于南海。

Lord Yu traced the Yellow River from Ji-shi, with the water channeled as far as Long-men. The water thence flew southwards to the north of mount Hua-shan; eastward then to the Di-zhu steadfast rock; eastward again to the ford of Meng-jin; eastward still to the junction and winding estuary area of the

Luo-shui River; and then onwards to the Da-pi-shan mountain. The Yellow River then flew northwards to pass the Jiang-shui River [in Xindu of Hebei], reaching the Da-lu-ze (continental [shelf]) lake. The Yellow River then continued north, where the water was divided and spread across the nine drainage rivers, and [near the coast] uniting again into the Ni-he (backflow; inverse welcoming reception per Yan Shigu) River [i.e., the conventional interpretation of a loop-like river which branched off in the upperstream before joining together at the lower stream, or the segment where the sea water and river water mixed together], the water entered the sea.

导河、积石，至于龙门；南至于华阴，东至于砥柱，又东至于孟津，东过洛汭，至于大伾；北过降水，至于大陆；又北，播为九河，同为逆河，入于海。

From the Bo-zhong-shan mountain Lord Yu traced the Yang-shui River [in Didao of Longxi], which, flowing eastwards, became the Han-shui River [south of the mountain of the Wu'guan Pass]. Farther flowing east, the flow became the water of the Cang-lang-shui River [southeast of mount Jingshan]; and after passing the San-shi (three river shores or three natural dykes; San-shi-shui River at Jingling per Yan Shigu), it went on to the Da-bie-shan mountain, flowing southwards where it entered the Jiang1-shui River. Continuing eastward, the water pooled together to form the Peng-li Lake; and from there its eastern flowing was to become the northern Jiang1-shui River, which entered the sea after that.

嶓冢导漾，东流为汉，又东，为沧浪之水，过三澨，至于大别，南入于江。东，汇泽为彭蠡，东，为北江，入于海。

From mount Min-shan Lord Yu traced and channeled the Ji-ang1-shui River, which, branching off to the east, formed the Tuo-shui (Te-shui per Yan Shigu) River, and flew eastward again to reach the Li-shui River. Passed the nine rivers' marshland, the water flew on to Dong-ling; then flowing east while slanted towards the north, the water converged in the loop area; and its eastern flow was the middle Jiang1-shui River, which entered the sea.

岷山导江，东别为沱，又东至于澧；过九江，至于东陵，东迆北，会于汇；东为中江，入于海。

Lord Yu traced the Yan3-shui water, which, flowing eastward, became the Ji-shui River. After the water entered the Yellow River, it flowed out to became the Xing-ze Lake. Flowing eastward to detour north of the Tao-qiu hill [at Dingtao of Shandong], the water flowed farther east to He[-ze] Lake. Then it went north-east, and united with the Wen-shui River; and thence it went north, and entered the sea to the east.

导沇水，东流为济，入于河，溢为荥；东出于陶丘北，又东至于菏，又东北，会于汶，又北，东入于海。

Lord Yu traced the Huai-shui from the Tong-bai-shan mountain. Flowing east, the water converged with the Si-shui and the Yih-shui Rivers, and flew eastward to enter the sea.

导淮自桐柏，东会于泗、沂，东入于海。

Lord Yu traced the Wei-shui from the Niao-shu-tong-xue mountain. Flowing eastward, the water converged with the Feng-shui River. Flowing eastwards it converged with the Jing-shui River. Farther east still, it passed the Qi-shui and the Ju1-shui Rivers, and then entered the Yellow River.

导渭自鸟鼠同穴，东会于沣，又东会于泾，又东过漆沮，入于河。

Lord Yu traced the Luo-shui from the Xiong-er-shan (bear ear) mountain. Flowing to the north-east, it united with the Jian-shui and the Chan-shui Rivers. Eastwards still, it united with the Yi-shui River. Then flowing northeastward, it entered the Yellow River.

导洛自熊耳，东北，会于涧、瀍；又东，会于伊，又东北，入于河。

CHAPTER V
THE FLOOD CONTROL FEATS

The section on the flood control's feats eulogized Lord Yu's accomplishment, i.e., settling the water and soils --which culminated in the nine prefectures being united, the nation's tax revenues collected, and the people enjoying their conferred surnames and fiefdoms. In *Shun-dian* (Lord Shun's commandments) of *Shang-shu*, Lord Shun was said to have constructed altars at the four corners of the world ('tan si-ao'), made sacrifice at the four seas ('chen si-hai') and made conferrals on twelve mountains ('feng shi-you-er shan').

> Thus the nine prefectures were effected a similar order; and the four corners (habitable lands in four directions per Yan Shigu) of the world ('si-ao') were made habitable. The nine mountains were cleared of their superfluous wood and sacrificed to ['lv-ji', namely, being erected the wood landmarks and launched a mountain road path as part of the sacrifice activities]; the sources of the nine rivers ('jiu chuan') were cleared; the nine lakes were well banked; and the tribute-bearer people from the four seas could then converge together [onto the nation's capital city in Jizhou the Great Xia land]. The six magazines (of material wealth including water, fire, metal, wood, mud and grains) were fully attended to; the different fields of the country were subjected to surrender of taxation revenue; the materials (i.e., grains) and revenues to be surrendered were diligently and carefully classified, with the principle laid out to be all meted out the taxation amount in reference to the three grades of the soil; and hence the centric nation ('zhong bang', i.e., the lord's Great Xia nation) was replete with the tax revenues. Giving out the conferral of lands and surnames [to the vassals], the lord said,

"paying deference [to the son of heaven], the virtue of it was the utmost paramount quality, and it is thus expected that none [of you vassals] would act contrary to my practiced rules of conduct and teachings."

九州攸同，四隩既宅，九山刊旅，九川涤源，九泽既陂，四海会同。六府孔修，庶土交正，砥慎财赋，咸则三壤成赋。中邦锡土、姓，祗台德先，不距朕行。

CHAPTER VI
THE FIVE TRIBUTE REGIONS

The last section on the five tribute regions was a narrative on the reach of the lord's power and influence as measured by a radius distance consisting of five 500-league sectors from near to far, that were termed by the territories of Dian-fu (sovereign domain), Hou-du (nobles' domain), Sui-fu (pacified domain), Yao-fu (restraint domain), and Huang-du (remote wilderness).

The territory of five hundred leagues formed the 'dian-fu' sovereign domain near the lord's capital city districts. From the territory of the first hundred leagues, the revenues surrendered were the whole plant of the grains (i.e., ears with the stalks --with the stalks used for feeding horses and construction, etc.) and the husbandry feed grass; from the territory of the two hundred leagues [minus the first one hundred league territory], the revenues were the grains' ears and spikelet; from the territory of the three hundred leagues [minus first two hundred league territory], the revenues were the stalks ('gao jie', a kind of stalk mats for sacrifice; or the conventional interpretation of 'jie' as the shelled grains), plus the people's performing various compulsory services; from the territory of the four hundred leagues [minus the first three hundred league territory], the revenues were the [large amount] grains in the husk; and from the territory of the five hundred leagues [minus first four hundred league territory], the revenues were the [small amount] refined rice.

五百里甸服：百里赋纳总，二百里纳铚，三百里纳秸服，四百里粟，五百里米。

The territory of five hundred leagues beyond the five hundred league 'dian-fu' territory constituted the "chi-hou" nature nobles' domain of 'hou-fu'. The first one hundred league territory of it was occupied by the lord's high ministers and great officers ('cai', i.e., either the '*qing*' or '*da-fu*' ministers); the second hundred league territory of it was occupied by the principalities of the barons ('nan bang' --who worked on behalf of the centric state; or the ren-guo' fiefdoms in *Shi-ji*'s passage on *Yu Gong*); and the other three [taken to be a typo for two] hundred leagues of the remaining 'hou-fu' territory was occupied by the various other vassals and princes.

五百里侯服：百里采，二百里男邦，三百里诸侯。

Beyond the 'dian-fu' and 'hou-fu' territories would be the five hundred league 'sui-fu' peaceful and pacified domain. In the first three hundred leagues of the 'sui-fu' territory, they evaluated and cultivated the learnings and teachings of the lord; and in the other two hundred leagues, they shouldered the role of developing martial awe and defense on behalf of the lord.

五百里绥服：三百里揆文教，二百里奋武卫。

Beyond the 'dian-fu', 'hou-fu' and 'sui-fu' territories would be the five hundred league 'yao-fu' restraint domain. In the first three hundred leagues of the 'yao-fu' territory was the requirement of observing the lord's teachings ('yi2', a word interpreted as peaceful and quiet in *Yi Fa* [posthumous naming] of *Zhou Shu*; soundex of 'yi4' for easiness per Yan Shigu); and the other two hundred leagues of the 'yao-fu' territory was the requirement of observing the lord's penal laws ('cai4').

五百里要服：三百里夷，二百里蔡。

Beyond the 'dian-fu', 'hou-fu', 'sui-fu' and 'yao-fu' territories would be the five hundred league 'huang-fu' remote wilderness (i.e., erratic submission; or uncultivated and neglected per Ma Rong (A.D. 79-166)) domain. in the first three hundred leagues of the 'huang-fu' territory the requirement of maintaining the undisciplined (i.e., 'mann2' being soundex for 'mann4' per Ma Rong) submission to the lord; and the other two hundred leagues of the 'huang-fu' territory was the requirement of erratic submission of tributes and movement of dwelling places ('liu 2'; or the place of exile).

五百里荒服：三百里蛮，二百里流。

To the east, the lord's fame and teachings reached the seas; to the west, the lord's fame and teachings extended to the quick sands (i.e., the Kumtag); to the north and south, the lord's fame and teachings penetrated to the utmost limits of the north and south; and the influence filled up to the edge of the four seas. Lord Yu was awarded the black jade 'gui' [power instrument with a pointer and square base] [from Lord Yao as symbol of his ranking], with the announcement of the completion of the flood control work.

东渐于海，西被于流沙，朔南暨声教讫于四海。禹锡玄圭，告厥成功。

CHAPTER VII
CONCLUSIVE REMARKS

In conclusion, it could be said that *Yu Gong* (Lord Yu's Tributes) could be positively identified to be a book written before *Lv-shi Chun-qiu* for its adoption of the Jizhou prefecture as the No. 1 prefecture versus the Yuzhou prefecture adopted by the latter. More specifically, it was written prior to Zou Yan (Zou-zi, ? 305-240 B.C.)'s proposition of the nine greater prefectures. Shi Nianhai, who deduced that *Yu Gong* could be written by a Wei Principality person during Wei King Huichengwang (r. 370-335, 334-319 B.C.)'s reign, specifically 370-362 B.C., could be the person who made the closest estimate among all modern historians. *Yu Gong* apparently formed the basis of all geography-related writings, as seen in the mountain component of *Shan Hai Jing*, in Zou Yan's Greater Nine Prefectures' theory, and in *Mu-tian-zi Zhuan*, not to mention the later books of *Zhou Li*, *Yi Zhou Shu* and *Er Ya*.

The spatial and cosmological concepts of ancient China could further corroborate the sequence of the books written. First, the place naming in *Yao Dian* of *Shang-shu* were the direct feed into the mountain part of *Shan Hai Jing*. *Yao Dian* talked about the four corners of Yu-yi (meaning the later 'corner Yi barbarians', a place called 'Tang-gu' or the hot spring valley), Nan-jiao (the southern outskirts, with the 'jiao' word implying the later 'Jiao-zhi' [Cochin china] for the crossing toes), Mei-gu (i.e., Ming-gu or the darkness/sunset valley), and Shuo-fang (the northern domain, called by 'You-du' or the dark capital city). In the same article *Yao Dian*, there was reference to four places of exile for the evil tribes, namely, Youzhou (i.e., 'You-du'), Mt. Chong-shan, San-wei (i.e., three precarious mountains), and Mt. Yu-shan (i.e., feather mountain). Note that Youzhou or You-du was not listed as one of the nine ancient prefectures in *Yu Gong* or Lord Yu's Tributes. *Lv-shi Chun-qiu* adopted the terms of *Da-xia* [grand Xia land], Bei-hu [northern dwelling –which was taken to be a northern gate of southern China in *Shi-ji*], San-wei and Fu-mu for the four wilderness, while *Er Ya* used the terms of Guzhu, Bei-hu [northern dwelling], Xi-wangmu [queen mother of the west] and Ri-xia [under the sun] were the four wilderness.

The four corners and nine prefectures' concept of the late Warring States time period, with varying names of the same nature, such as 'liu sha' (quick sand, i.e., the Kumtag Desert) for the west and 'pan2 mu' (peach tree) or 'fu mu' (mulberry tree) for the east, developed to the philosophical concept *"liu he"* (*luhe*) to describe the world with four borders, a top [heaven] and a bottom [earth] by the time of the Qin state's unification of China in 221 B.C. *Lv-shi Chun-qiu*, a Qin dynasty book, in the *You Shi3* [having a beginning] chapter, talked about the nine prefectures on the land and the nine skies in the heaven, as well as the four seas with an east-west distance of 28000 leagues and a south-north distance of 26000 leagues, and the four 'si ji' or four polars (poles; struts; extremity; culmen per David Pankenier) with an east-west distance of 97000 leagues and a south-north distance of 97000 leagues. The usage of the number 'nine' could be said to be a fuzzy philosophical concept, not a specific designation. Among the nine [greater or not] prefectures and the nine skies, there was a centric block [with the neatly-included Horn, Neck and Root mansions] or 'jun-tian' central high sky, plus eight quarters of the astral skies --which was different from the four quarters of the astral skies named after the azure dragon, the black tortoise-snake, the white tiger and the vermilion bird, nor the twelve sector divisions of the ecliptic -- that often saw one lunar mansion spreading across two sector divisions of the ecliptic. (*Huai Nan Zi*, in its astronomy/astrology section, had a second discourse on the nine concentric and/or spherical skies, termed 'jiu chong' or nine spheres of Heaven, which miraculously matched with 6-7 Paradiso cantiche in Dante Alighieri's *Divine Comedy*.)

Ai Nanying (A.D. 1583 - 1646) of the Ming dynasty, i.e., author of *Yu Gong Tu Zhu* (Commentary on the *Yu Gong* Map), considered *Yu Gong* as the progenitor of all geographic texts both ancient and modern. The territory described by *Yu Gong* fell within Sinitic China's outer limits, namely, the middle mountain ranges and partial segments of the northern and western mountain ranges, but not beyond the Wangwu-shan and Yanmen-zhi-shan mountains to the north, or the Bozhong-shan mountain to the west. This geographical delimitation, when combined with the astrological mapping of the stars of the twenty-eight lunar mansions, shaped the perpetuating theme of Sinitic China's centric status as the country of rituals and civilization versus the barbarians. This arrogant mindset, which was built on top of the ancient Chinese pride in the Sinitic language, culture, rituals, rites and protocols, turned out to be fatal to the Sinitic nation at the Age of Discovery, when the villages of earth could no longer be isolated from each other.

AFTERWORD: INTRODUCTION TO *THE SINITIC CIVILIZATION*

The *Afterword* of this book is from *Introduction* to *The Sinitic Civilization Book I* (ISBN: 978-1-5320-5828-8) and *Book II* (ISBN: 978-1-5320-5830-1), which is an overview of the Sinitic civilization that could serve as complimentary reading for *Tribute of Yu*. The *Introduction* was added to the duology after receiving critique from Daniel Patrick Morgan, a student of Professor Edward L. Shaughnessy. Daniel questioned how this duology is different from or better than Jacques Gernet (1921-2018)'s *A History of Chinese Civilization* (*Le Monde Chinois*, 1972/1999) or Needham's *Science and Civilization* series. Daniel pointed out that the body texts went into far more details about certain historical events, technical matters (astronomy), and scholarly arguments (archeo-astronomy, and the authenticity of sources) than did a shorter, standard introduction such as Gernet's. From the calendrical perspective, Daniel kindly perused the related contents as to the ancient Chinese calendars, felt that the author was "operating within the limits" and advised the author to be "cautious about certain connections and interpretations". Daniel saw the impreciseness of this duology as to its placement between genres: somewhere between such an introduction like Gernet's and a greater over-arching argument about Chinese civilization, such as seen in the Needham's. Daniel has valid questions as to the "genre, aims, intended readership, relation with other works", etc.

Since the preface(s) to the duology *The Sinitic Civilization* did not answer some of the above questions, an introduction is provided here to answer the issues raised by Daniel and to cover the duology books' scope, thesis, purpose and limitations. This

Introduction would go beyond the purpose of a book introduction to cover some additional topics such as divination, i.e., the Sinitic nation's structural and cultural backbone. First we want to make a point that the duology on the Sinitic civilization and history could not be anywhere close to Joseph Needham's *Science and Civilization* series. Needham's *Science and Civilization* series is a general history book on China covering the science and technology aspects. This duology's main technical coverage was the threading-together and synthesis of ancient China's calendrical history, i.e., topics that could be elusive to ordinary readers who did not have the luxury to peruse the ancient Chinese classics. The calendrical matter is scattered in different contexts of the two books, with discourses on Lord Yao's commandments and the 366-day calendar in Chapter 8 of *Book One*, and discourses on the *Zhuanxu-li*, *Taichu-li* and *Sifen-li* calendars in Chapters 26, 32 and 40 of *Book Two* [plus a section on Liu Xin's *Santong-li* calendar in Chapter 35]. The important points to make here in regard to the calendrical matter are that the five planets' records and the sexagenary reign years as seen in the forgery contemporary version of *The Bamboo Annals* could be merely flashback results; the ancient quarter remainder calendars' mechanism could be discovered after the rule of thumbs in regards to the 81 '*ri fa*' (diurnal) number and the leap month intercalation, i.e., to place seven intercalary months within 19 years [which had 235 calendar months], was discovered; and the sexagesimal system of sixty years possibly started in the 4th century B.C., about one or two sexagenary cycles or one Jupiter chronogram ahead of invention of the Qin state's *Zhuanxu-li* calendar (247 B.C.). Half a century ago, Professor Jacques Gernet already pointed out that "the cycle of sixty was only applied to the years ... from the second century B.C. onwards." The five planets' data could be seen in *Wu-xing Zhan*, a book that logged the planets' movements from the late Qin dynasty onward, and it would be in the late Han dynasty that the data on the seven luminaries [including sun and moons] were seen in the Han dynasty '*chen-wei*' category prophecy books.

Technology and science wise, the pre-2000 B.C copper-based metallurgy was discussed in *Book I* without making conclusive statements on its indigenousness versus the possibility as an import. In regards to bronze, Jacques Gernet had a brilliant point about the continuity of the Lungshan black pottery and the bronze vessels of the Shang period. Gernet, who took Hsia (Xia) "very probable the existence of this dynasty" for the traces of "the first city-palaces and the first manifestations of Chinese civilization to the end of the third millennium", pointed out that the Shang dynasty and the earlier Lungshan (Longshan) Culture exhibited a direct succession, as represented in the "very typical shapes which appear in closely related versions both in the fine black pottery of Shantung (Lungshan) and in the bronze vessels of the Shang period". Gernet, half a century ago, derived the brilliant conclusion that "the mastery of the potters of Lungshan, the high temperatures which they seem to have been capable of obtaining, and the restricted role of hammering and forging in the technical traditions of the Far East all incline one to favor the idea of an independent discovery of bronze metallurgy". This viewpoint, from a different angle, invalidated the claim that the Indo-Europeans gave China the bronze technology or the Sumerians gave China the oracle bone scripts.

The Shang bronze vessels, like the Shang oracle bones and tortoise shells, carried the sparsely-written characters that denoted the emblems, names and titles, developed to the bronzeware inscription with hundreds of characters by the Zhou dynasty, the moon phase information of which could be the sole extant data to periodize the reign years of ancient dynasties and kings. In Chapter 19 of *Book I*, there is a discourse on Zhang Wenyu's consistent "fixed points" interpretation of bronzeware moon phases and his rebuttal of the 1-2 day floating deviation, the 3-day floating deviation [as proposed by 20th century historian Dong Zuobin] and the 7-day floating deviation [as proposed by Wang Guowei]. The scientific contents were also briefly touched on in *Book II* in the context of discussing Han Dynasty King Huai'nan (Liu An) and his book *Wan*

Bi Shu (techniques with ten thousand pieces in one complete compendium) as well as in the context of discussing the divination topics related to Han Dynasty scholar Zhang Heng, i.e., author of *Ling Xian* (supernatural {celestial bodies' orbit} chart). Gernet succinctly noted that the Chinese logic "followed the path taken by the specialists in divination, who were the founding fathers of mathematics in the Chinese world. The manipulation of numbers and the combination of signs suited to translate the correct values of space-time were to serve as the basis of philosophical theories and of the sciences." Gernet meant that the Chinese dialectics was "a kind of sophistry which is quite original in character and distinguished by its essentially pragmatic aim from that of the Greek world, which was bound up with the practice of making speeches in law courts and political assemblies" and that the Chinese, after a short dialectic excursion, reverted back to the old 'divinatory' tradition, which was dichotomy. Gernet's point about divination and science was very much corroborated by the two Han dynasty books of *Wan Bi Shu* (techniques with ten thousand pieces in one complete compendium) and *Ling Xian* (supernatural {celestial bodies' orbit} chart).

Since divination was intrinsically-related to the divine spirits, ancestor worship and theology, as well as the Sinitic language spawning and nation building, it deserves a highlighted discourse in this *Introduction*. Ancient divination, which ran parallel with the tortoise shell divination and yarrow divination in the Zhou dynasty, developed to the occult "*Shu-shu Jia*" (Techniques and Calculations) school in the Han dynasty, that encompassed astronomy, calendrical ephemeris, five constant elements, tortoise shell divination and yarrow divination, miscellaneous prognostication, and forms and names (i.e., the Logicians) and engendered the "*chen-wei*' esoteric commentaries of the five classics. The *Zhou-yi* divination's binary system was acknowledged to be the foundation for the arithmetic language of modern computers. Gottfried Wilhelm von Leibniz (1646-1716), who took the Chinese male-female system as corresponding to his zero and one binary system, might not have realized that it was the earlier Jesuits who brought back the Sinitic divinatory philosophy, and later in his late years, wrote *Discourse on the Natural Theology of the Chinese* in acknowledgment of debts the West owed to ancient China.

Divination, i.e., the Sinitic nation's structural and cultural backbone, could be traced to the Jiahu civilization (7000-8000 B.C; dendrochronologically-adjusted 7500 - 8800 B.C.) which could be the source feed for the Lingjiatan civilization (6000 B.C.) in the lower Huaishui River rivercourse and the Dawenkou and Longshan culture in the lower Yellow River rivercourse. The Jiahu site, taken to be of the Peiligang Culture type, produced the earliest tortoise shells containing dice-like stones, which could be the origin of Sinitic China's tortoise shell divination. The Lingjiatan civilization, which produced the octagram star (i.e., prototyped on top of the pottery spin wheels), the double eagle-head jade octagram (i.e., prototyped on top of the three-leg or three-head sun bird of the Neolithic time, as seen in the excavated potteries carrying the three-leg birds coupled with the sun image or the three-head birds pulling the sun in the middle of its joint body), and a jade turtle with eight-trigrams-like drawings on a jade plate inside of its belly, corroborated the Jiahu site's religious nature of the prehistoric tortoise shell divination. The tortoise shell divination, which was absent along the Yangtze and southern China but widely seen in the Peiligang and Dawenkou cultures, exhibited itself as a patented Sinitic tradition. Though, the tortoise shell divination was infrequently seen in the successor Longshan culture sites and the Xia dynasty sites, only to be revived again starting from the Lower Phase II of the Erligang site of the Shang dynasty.

Archeological data showed the wide usage of bone divination among the Yangshao Culture sites of the upper, middle and lower Yellow River rivercourse 6000 years ago, including the sheep's scapula with burnt marks in the third phase Yangshao culture site of Xiawanggang (lower king's hill) in Xichuan of Xiachuan, Henan; sheep, pig and cattle bones in the Majiayao site of Shiling (stony ridge) in Fujiamen of Wushan, Gansu; and deer and sheep bones in the Fuhegoumen (rich river ditch gate) site of Inner Mongolia. This could be a matter of sourcing of divination materials when the Sinitic people expanded to northwestern China and the northern frontier. The Longshan (Lungshan) culture along the middle Yellow River rivercourse, which could be related to the Jiahu Culture's eastern infusion towards the Dawenkou Culture and its subsequent back-tracing westward, and the successive Xia and Shang dynasties, inherited the Yangshao bone divination tradition, with the Shang people perfecting the divination custom of osteogenesis in addition to reviving the tortoise shell divination. In the opinion of Zhang Zhongpei (1934-2017, curator of the forbidden city museum), bone divination was a universalized religion of prehistoric Sinitic China. (Zhang Deshui and Li Lina of the Museum of Henan Province claimed that prehistoric China possessed a third jade divination as seen in the Hongshan culture in Northeast China, the Liangzhu culture [of the Austronesian people] in the Taihu Lake basin, and the Lingjiatan culture in Anhui. The jade divination of the middle and late Neolithic period should be properly termed "jade as burial" and "jade as sacrifice", a practice seen in the Shimao Culture of northwestern China and Sanxingdui Culture of the Sichuan basin to the west as well as inherited by the Xia and Shang China dynasties. *Tai-bu* of *Zhou-li*, a book compiled by Liu Xin (50 B.C.- 23 A.D.), claimed that imperial sorcerer Tai-bu of the ancient times had three prognostication methods of using cracked jade (*yu zhao*), cracked title (*wa zhao*) and cracked fields (*yuan zhao*). The cracked jade (*yu zhao*) was interpreted by Zheng Xuan (A.D. 127-200) of the Latter Han dynasty to be about examining the tortoise shell's cracked veins which were similar to a jade's veins.)

Prehistoric Sinitic China possibly developed trigrams and hexagrams on top of the tortoise shell divination and bone divination. In Neolithic Jiahu, the burial of stone-embedded tortoise shells started with two, four, six, and eight and progressed toward the direction of one and two, namely, some divination experiments towards a manageable numerological target. The Lingjiatan jade turtle, with an octagonal plate sandwiched between the jade tortoise shell and the carapace of the jade tortoise, appeared to be a set of divination tools that had the rudimentary shape of eight trigrams, i.e., what Han dynasty history book *Shi-ji* defined the function of divination as setting the four [sky] nets (i.e., dimensions) at four corners and aligning the eight trigrams within each other's sight. As pointed out by Zhang Zhenglang (1912-2005), Neolithic China already possessed trigrams and hexagrams, as seen in the Qingdun site of the Songze Culture (5400-4400 B.C.) in Hai'an of Jiangsu, which produced eight carved bone inscriptions showing the existence of six 'yao' trigrams, such as 353364 ('*dun*' hexagram [with '*gen*' and '*qian*' trigrams] in *Zhou Yi*) and 623531 ('*gui-mei*' hexagram [with '*dui*' and '*zhen*' trigrams; disputed to be '*da-zhuang*' hexagram by Wu Yong of Huazhong Normal University] in *Zhou Yi*). Wu Yong, in analyzing the excavated Neolithic trigrams and hexagrams, expressed doubt about applying the reading of Shang oracle bone and bronzeware pictographs to identifying the prehistoric carved characters. Wu Yong pointed out that the digits on the Neolithic trigrams and hexagrams, i.e., 3, 4, 5 and 6 in "353364" or 1, 2, 3, 5 and 6 in "623531", were actually either male-female (i.e., odd-even) images (that formed the resulting six-liners) of the divinatory texts or four symbols, that were for the binary divination system but were misread as decimal numbers 1 to 9. Without expounding the difference of five versus four Neolithic 'signs' as seen on the Qingdun bones, Wu Yong believed that the four-sign milfoil system (i.e., "senior male"; "senior female"; "junior female"; and "junior male"), when raised to the power of six, yielded the more manageable set of 4096 six-liner dictums --which were the 4096 poems (64x64 six-liners) in Jiao Yanshou's *Jiao-shi Yi-lin* (forest of *The Book of Changes*).

Not to make this *Introduction* into a discourse on divination, the above elaboration's point was that Sinitic China had a divinatory history of more than 8000 years, with the Sinitic written language very much a resultant or byproduct invention. After prehistoric Sinitic China developed trigrams and hexagrams from the tortoise shell divination and bone divination, trigrams and hexagrams possibly evolved to milfoil divination using yar-rows independently of the tortoise shell divination and bone divination. Interpretation books related to *Zhou-yi* (i.e., *The Book of Changes*) claimed that it was the [fabled] ancient sovereign Fu-xi who designed the eight trigrams by examining the heaven and earth; and Sima Qian's *Shi-ji* claimed that Zhou founder-king Wenwang, when imprisoned in a place called Youli, renovated the ancient eight trigrams into sixty-four hexagrams. Gernet suc-cinctly pointed out that in Zhou China, "divination itself devel-oped autonomously in the time of the first kings of Chou" in the direction of the yarrow stems instead of "divination by fire" of Shang China. Though, milfoil divination, i.e., numerical stalk divination, could have already existed before the Zhou dynasty. Oracle bone expert Tang Lan ascertained some Shang dynasty "*shi1-shu*" numerical stalk divination signs on the Sipanmo div-ination bone, which were written as "787676 called kui [with the fief signific], and 757566 called kui [with the Dipper signific]". The com-bination 'kui-kui', in the Latter Han dynasty, became the name of the Fiery Thearch. Not going into details here about Fu-xi being a fable figure of the Han dynasty and being prototyped on the Shang dynasty's wind god, ancient China could have developed the trigrams through astronomical observation. In the Qingtai (green terrace) site of Xingyang, about the same spot where Johan Gunnar Andersson discovered the Yangshao civilization, there was exca-vated in year 2015 a yellow mud underground terrace with nine pottery jars surrounding it, with the 5500-year-old jars specu-lated to be related to ancient Chinese's divinatory reverence for the Northern Dipper (i.e., Ursa Major) and its handle.

Zuo Zhuan (Zuo-qiu-ming's commentary on *Chun Qiu*) and *Guo Yu* (discourse of the states) carried twenty-two divination cases that showed the juxtaposition of two divinatory methods of the tortoise shell divination and milfoil divination via the "*shi1-shu*" numbers, with the former given more weight over the latter in the augury process for its possibly high "matched divination" and "realized divination" rate. Though, Neolithic [or Shang China's] milfoil divination could be just simple, or original, or root hexagrams, as pointed out by Wu Yong, and might not be of the nature of root versus resultant (alternative, transformant) hexagrams of *Zhou-yi* of the Zhou dynasty. The simple, or original, or root hexagrams were seen in the fabled alternative divination of *Lian-shan Yi* and *Gui-cang Yi* as seen in the A.D. 279 Ji-zhong tomb, or the excavated 1993 Wangjiatai divination bamboo slips, or the *Shi-fa* (stalk) divination slips. The *Zhou-yi* divination system with the complex change mechanisms might not have a fixed rule or method according to the caveat statement in Lu Lord Zhaogong's 12th year of *Zuo Zhuan*, namely, the divination should not be canonized or essentialized as long as it fit the change [of circumstances]. The "change", namely, "conversion" or not of a hexagram in *Zhou Yi*, was something that could be interpreted to be the result of human, natural or supernatural influence.

Divination with trigrams and hexagrams is an occult science that the barbarians, whom were described by Sima Qian [or Chu Shaosun] in *Gui-ce Lie-zhuan* of *Shi-ji* to have their separate tortoise shell divination and bone divination, never mastered. Divination played the role of a repository recording the prehistoric Sinitic history. Li Pingxing, an early communist who was a preparatory Soviet government commissariat member at one time during the 1927 Nanchang mutiny, pointed out that the *Zhou Yi* divination was an "argot language" history. The twenty-two divination cases as recorded in *Zuo Zhuan* and *Guo Yu* are scattered across the duology books. In Chapter 23 of *Book I*, there is a section on "The Yarrow & Turtle Divination Mechanism of the Shang, Zhou & Chu People", in which Soong dynasty scholar Zhu Xi's seven rules of prognostication and modern scholar Gao Heng's predicate logic interpretation method are discussed. In Chapter 25 of *Book II*, there is discussion of '[Yi-]dao' (i.e., the divination way) in the *Yi* 'zhuan', namely, ten interpretation books for the *Yi* divination, and Confucius' 'tian dao' (heavenly way), i.e., the philosophical divination. As to the fabled alternative divination of *Lian-shan Yi* and *Gui-cang Yi* as seen in the A.D. 279 Ji-zhong tomb, or the excavated 1993 Wangjiatai divination bamboo slips, or the *Shi-fa* (stalk) divination slips, there are dedicated Chapters 36 and 37 of *Book II* dealing with those divinatory topics in the context of interpreting *Shan Hai Jing* ('The Classics of Mountains and Seas'), a book that was dramatized by Gao Xingjian, the Year 2000 Nobel Prize winner and a 'pretender' who misinterpreted the Sinitic genesis and Mankind creation theories.

Back to the theme of this *Introduction*. This duology is not a general history like Gernet's book but could serve the purpose of filling in "gaps, imperfections, and errors" that were said by Gernet to be inevitable in his general history due to the fact that China's written literature contained "rich and varied a range of events extending over three and a half millennia". Gernet's *A History of Chinese Civilization* (*Le Monde Chinois*, 1972/1999) is a general history book on China, that covers the political, economic, and social aspects and traverses the Chinese history from antiquity down to the 20th century. This author's duology on the Sinitic civilization and history, however, covered the time span of history of the Sinitic civilization from antiquity, to the 3rd millennium B.C. to A.D. 85, with the scope being the enumeration and synthesis of historical facts. Hence the duology carries the subtitle of a factual history. The duology's timeframe falls into what Charles Hucker (1919-1994) termed by the formative age (from antiquity to the 3rd century B.C.) and the early imperial age (from the 3rd century B.C. to the 10th century A.D.). In regards to Daniel's questions as to the "genre, aims, intended readership, relation with other works", etc., the duology could be considered a quasi-general history book for readers who wish to gain a better understanding of ancient China beyond the generalized and universally accepted conclusions. This could be achieved through digestion of primitive data presented in this duology, rather second-hand enumeration of facts, and via comparison with more than Gernet's book to include Charles Hucker's *China's Imperial Past: An Introduction to Chinese History and Culture* (Stanford University Press, 1975).

Gernet piled praise on the Chinese civilization for the "tremendous historical dimension", "writing, its technology, its conceptions of man and of the world, its religions and its political institutions", and "the originality of all Chinese intellectual traditions". Specifically, Gernet raised a good point in regards to importance of intellectuals who had "the prerogative of the written word in the Chinese world" and who were "attached in China to a knowledge of writing and to book knowledge" and acknowledged the Chinese language characterset as "most effective instruments of political unification". Note that Hucker's *China's Imperial Past* did not shake off the old-fashioned stereotyped description of China and its land, topology, people, language and other "themes that pervade Chinese life and history", such as China proper and its purported insulation from "other major centers of civilization until the advent of modern communication and transport techniques" or China taken to be the "only major nation of Asia that is racially homogeneous". The limitations or demerits of this duology are lack of synthesis of subjects on a chapter scale. In contrast, Hucker's book, in addition to a general history, aligned the chapters into political institutions, socioeconomic organization, religion and thought, and literature and the arts. Though, this duology could serve the purpose of a complimentary reading to Gernet's Chinese history book in that it filled the "gaps, imperfections, and errors" of both Gernet's and Hucker's works.

Comparisons could be illustrated to make a point about the utility of this duology as far as aims, intended readership, and relation with other works are concerned. Armed with the historical facts presented in this duology, readers, who had previously read Gernet's book or Hucker's book, could come to a different understanding of China's history. For example, Hucker categorically claimed that the Chinese society consisted of "at least 80 per cent of the total population" that consisted of "farming villagers" and "20 per cent or so of the traditional population" of the "homogeneous literate culture'. This categorization is similar to

Alfred Tennyson and William A. P. Parsons Martin's claims as to "A Cycle of Cathay" for Sinitic China's superficial staleness, namely, what Gernet pointed out to be the repeat of stages of "stagnation, periodical return to a previous condition, and permanence of the same social structures and the same political ideology". As pointed out by Jacques Gernet, China was a technical civilization, not a vegetable (i.e., agrarian) civilization as commonly perceived, and took China as "the land of the most skilled metallurgists". It needs to be acknowledged that Professor Jacques Gernet was the most brilliant Sinologist of all, who made almost impeccable generalizations about history of China and must had influenced Daniel Patrick Morgan as to the choice of his subject of studies. Perhaps, a student of Chinese history could read both Professor Jacques Gernet's book and this duology to achieve an enhanced understanding of the Chinese history. Namely, this duology plays the role of compensating for the "gaps, imperfections, and errors" as far as historical facts are concerned.

Though, Gernet, who was the most prescient among all Sinologists, made some similar general observations, such as the argument that "no clergy, no military caste, no merchant class ever succeeded in gaining political power" in China while applying the term of Sino-barbarian autocracy to the southern and northern dynasties (A.D. 590-755) of China, a time period of disintegration for China, that saw northern China being ruled by the Shatuo Turks who belonged to a mercenary military caste. Gernet's prescience in evaluating China's imperial system could be seen in his caution to avoid making distinction between "monarchy and democracy too absolute", and expressed admiration for the "complex forms of political organization" of China and "fundamental traditions" in the political, religious, aesthetic, juridical arena. Gernet erred in claiming that the "peasant militias", i.e., Soviet-sponsored proxies, founded in 1949 the communist nation after sweeping away "a military dictatorship", i.e., Republic of China. Gernet did not know that it was the Soviet-supplied artillery divisions and regiments that blasted the cities of Jinzhou,

Xinbao'an, Taiyuan and Tientsin to pieces. Gernet thought he had worked out "a general framework" that "will help to crystallize... ideas about the successive changes in the political forms of the Chinese world". Note that the communist revolution of China was not another indigenous or autochthonous cycle of 50 years in Cathay. In the following, the scope, thesis, purpose and limitations of the duology will be elaborated and contrasted with Gernet's book in a parallel framework.

This duology is sequentially aligned in the format of a comprehensive and factual recital of dynasty-by-dynasty chronicles that are mainly based on the ancient annals of *Shi-ji* (Historian's Records), *The Spring & Autumn Annals*, and *The Bamboo Annals*, with contents covering the topics of archaeology, bronzeware, astronomy, divination, and calendar interspersed throughout. The duology on the Sinitic civilization and history started with Chapter 1 entitled *"Asking Heaven"* ("Heavenly Questions") which was an ancient Chinese epic with a hybrid of questions about the riddles and enigma concerning the Universe, Genesis, Nature, and the rise and fall of dynasties. This epic contains the untainted theological and cosmological framework of ancient China, such as the rainhat-shaped round heaven and square earth, the skies being propped up by eight pillars (*'ba zhu'*), and the celestial hub (*'wo* [rotating] *wei* [heavenly net]') with the heavenly polar(s) subjoined to the celestial body by an axial rope. The pillar concept could have origin in Zhou King Wuwang's poem called *Zhi* (pillars of the sky), which stated that the sky's pillars could not be damaged, and if damaged, could not be repaired by the human force. In Zou Yan (Tsou Yen) or his disciples' works, the pillars were described to be located in the connection area of heaven and earth in the far way areas (*'tian-di ji'*) of the remaining eight 'greater' prefectures [beyond the Centric "Greater" Prefecture]. Hucker, who possibly took the Chinese as atheists since antiquity, claimed that "the Chinese felt no need to explain the creation of the universe and the origin of mankind". Actually, ancient China merely lacked a personified omnipotent, omniscient and omnipresent god who created the universe and engendered the mankind, and stratified the divine spirits into the grandiose sky (*'huang tian'*) and the lord on high (*'shang di'*) before combining the two into one and creating a separate grand one god (*'tai yi'*) by the late Zhou dynasty.

In *Book I*, in addition to the epic *Heavenly Questions* (Chapter 1), two chapters are dedicated to interpreting the ancient classic, including a complete exposition on geography book *Yu Gong* (Lord Yu's Tributes; Tribute of Yu) in Chapter 20, and a write-up on fiction *Mu-tian-zi Zhuan* (Zhou King Muwang's Travelogue) in Chapter 21. *Lord Yu's Tributes*, which talked about Lord Yu's flood control and zoning of the nine prefectures of Sinitic China, was the cornerstone on which the Sinitic nation, with the three successive dynasties of Xia, Shang and Zhou from the same big family, was founded, and the blueprint according to which the imperial administrative layout was mapped throughout the past millennia. *Zhou King Muwang's Travels* contained six travelogues that covered three discrete stories of no successive bearing to one another. The first four travelogues, i.e., visit with Count of the Yellow River at today's northeastern Yellow River Bend, travel to mount Kunlun [where the Yellow Thearch's palaces and Feng-long's tomb were], rendezvous with Queen Mother of the West, and three months' hunting at the northern feather wilderness, were about longevity, immortality and divination; the 5th travelogue was about hunting and divination around the Eastern Zhou capital district area on the false assumption that the Western Zhou kings had already relocated eastward, a symptom of retrograde amnesia; and the last travelogue was about the mourning customs of the Zhou dynasty, which was a subject of the later Han dynasty book called *The Book of Rites*.

The chapters of this duology are arranged in sequence of the ages sorted by the dynasties and kings or emperors, and put under the topical sections of prehistory, Xia, Shang, Zhou, Qin and Han dynasties. Instead of outlining a summary of each chapter in this Introduction, a quick overview will be given here. The second section of *Book I*, from Chapters 2 to 6, covers China's prehistory that is examined through the angles of archaeology, genetic research, ancient literature and fables. The three dimensional validation approach, i.e., underground/archaeological excavated artifacts and astronomical/calendrical data, is adopted for ascertaining the historical truth recorded in the history annals, real or forged, which should have filled in the "gaps, imperfections, and errors" that Gernet felt were left open in his history book. The next three sections detailed the history of the three Chinese dynasties of Xia, Shang and Zhou, with *Book I* ending in the late 7th century B.C., about the midpoint of the 242 years covered in Confucius' abridged book *The Spring & Autumn Annals* (722-481 B.C.). Throughout the duology and up to the interregnum (841-828 B.C. per *Shi-ji*/840-827 per Zhang Wenyu), the forgery contemporary version of *The Bamboo Annals*, with its forgery contents covering the prehistoric legendary thearchs before the three dynasties of Xia (Chapters 10-12), Shang (Chapters 13-15) and Zhou (Chapters 16-23), was debunked line by line.

For China's prehistory, note the overwhelming evidence that the ruins or origin of majority of the ancient thearchs from the pre-Xia dynasty eras, such as the Zhu-rong Ruins (in the Zheng state), the Tai-hao Ruins (in the Chen-guo state), Taichen {Shang Dynasty} Ruins (in the Soong state), the Zhuanxu Ruins (in the Wey state), You-shen (in the Wey state), the Kunwu Ruins (in the Wey state), Chu-qiu Ruins (in the Wey state), and Shao-hao Ruins (in the Lu state), were located along the middle Yellow River line and corroborated the O3a1c-002611 haplogroup Sinitic people's same origin in the central plains of North China. Whether Sinitic China ever had an earlier united kingdom (or dynasty) than Xia was unknown. However, archaeological excavations showed that over six thousand years ago, the Chinese continent entered a jade age from the Mesolithic age, with unison jade ritual artifacts (such as the square-shaped 'yu-cong' jade disks with a round cylindrical solid body and an inner perforated round hole and the jade hatchets) adopted in different regions, albeit the co-existence of regionally-differentiated potteries at the non-rulers' or plebeian levels. The Sinitic civilization's contribution to the world should not be underestimated. Since remote antiquity, at least over 10,000 years ago, there was the spread of North China's microlithic stone tools towards the west. This was followed by the spread of the 6000-year-old Lingjiatan double-eagle-head jade octagram to Central Asia, an ancient emblem built on top of the octagram star that had origin in the Sinitic pottery spin wheels with a history of 12,000-15,000 years. Additionally, there was the spread to Central Asia of the patented Sinitic gourd-shaped colored and red potteries with a beam neck.

Gernet made a succinct point that the West or the world "borrowed from China" without "realizing it" nor "recognizing its sizable debt to her, but for which we ourselves would not be what we are". This is similar to Aly Mazaheri's claim in *La Route De La Soie* (1983) that China just needed the Ferghana stallions while the West needed everything from China, including products such as paper, musk, iron cast ovens, iron wok, steel nails, pliers, needles, scissors, iron file, iron hammers, bronze mirrors, fire-making sickle [that Europe had utilized for eighteen centuries], etc. What Gernet and Mazaheri did not realize was Sinitic China's prehistoric contribution, including the written language and the cognates. It would not be farfetched to make a claim that the Sinitic pictographic characters, which could have origin in the Jiahu pristine engraved pictograms with a long history of 6000-8000 years, was the common origin for both the Shang oracle bone characters and the Sumerian wedge script --that shared similar significs or radicals, such as using the 'bow' signific for armies, adopting the reeds' signific to mean writing, and treating the 'square earth' character as animal, hunting and husbandry. In addition, it could be deduced that the Sinitic language, which shared 74% cognates with the Proto-Tibeto-Burman, could be the source for both the cognates of the Proto-North-Caucasian and the Proto-Indo-European for the "Old Chinese" sharing 43% cognates with the Proto-North-Caucasian, rather 23% with the Proto-Indo-European --as a result of the N haplogroup people's relocating to North Asia and then to Scandinavia and bringing along the Sinitic language to the Proto-North-Caucasian who in turn gave it to the Proto-Indo-European. From the bronze technology angle, Jacques Gernet believed that the Chinese "mastery of the potters of Lungshan, the high temperatures which they seem to have been capable of obtaining, and the restricted role of hammering and forging in the technical traditions of the Far East all incline one to favor the idea of an independent discovery of bronze metallurgy".

Sima Qian's *Shi-ji* claimed that the three dynasties of Xia, Shang and Zhou came from the same family, i.e., descendants of the Yellow Thearch. Existence of the first Chinese dynasty of Xia was doubted by the academics as a result of lack of evidence of written language characterset that could serve as an intermediary for transitioning to the Shang dynasty oracle bones. Whether Xia possessed a written language or not, *Jinn Yu* of *Guo Yu* (discourse of the states) claimed that the Yang-ren people, namely, the Yang-fan people near the Xia people's You-Xia-zhi-ju habitat, carried the Xia and Shang dynasties' legacy classics. The successor Shang people, in history, held the role as the custodian of the thearchs, for which they were said to be in possession of books: '*you* [having] *ce* [threaded documents] *you* [having] *dian* [canons]'. There is speculation that the Xia kings were the same as the Shang kings but were manufactured by the Zhou dynasty people to justify succeeding the mandate of heaven from the ancestral Xia people while not having discernment that the Xia dynasty suffered a period of loss of the kingdom as a result of usurpation of the Xia thrones by Hou-yi and Han-zhuo, a theme widely covered in the epic *Heavenly Questions*. The Xia kings versus the Shang kings, like the Shang kings versus the Zhou kings, could be an in-law relationship or an endogamy-turned coup according to historian Kwang-chih Chang. Zhang Junshi pointed out that Xia Kings Taikang, Zhongkang and Shaokang possessed the Shang-style '*geng*' stem; Xia King Di-zhu, who was known as Di-ning, carried the '*ding*' stem; and last Xia King Jie was known to have the '*gui*' stem.

Kwang-chih Chang took the Shang kings' '*jia*', '*yi*' versus '*ding*' bifurcated groups as some kind of in-law relationship serving the endogamy purpose.

Zhou China, taken to be the dynasty that had expanded Sinitic China's historical boundary to what it was like at the time the Qin empire reunited China, could have actually inherited Shang China's territories, with the difference being the level of exercise of control over the territories. The Zhou people called their country by '*qu-xia*' (regional/minor Xia), a term juxtaposed against '*kuang-xia*' (grandiose Xi) or '*shi-xia*' (prevalent Xia). The Zhou people, on basis of the ancient poems *Shi-jing*, had constant battles and fights against the Rong & Di people, namely, the Haplogroup O3a2c1*-M134 and O3a2c1a-M117 people known as the historical Qiang and Hu barbarians or what Zhou King Jing[3]wang termed by the Tao-wu northwestern barbarian exiles. *Zuo Zhuan*, in Lu Lord Zhaogong's 9th year, carried Zhou King Jing[3]wang (r. 544-520 B.C.)'s rebuke to the Jinn state in regards to inviting the barbarians to the Zhou capital city district area to harm the Zhou people and implied that the Zhou people, together with a batch of the same Ji-surnamed states, had received the conferral of fiefs in the western territories from the Xia king(s) for agricultural minister Hou-ji's contribution, with the list of the states including the Wei-guo state and the Rui-guo state along the Yellow River Bend. Unlike the laconic inscription of the Shang bronzeware, Zhou China, for its abundant production of bronzeware artifacts carrying munificent description of events related to religion, war, administration, life and judicia, etc., and for the extant history annals *Zuo Zhuan*, presented us all-encompassing picture of a brilliant autochthonous culture of East Asia with vivid political, religious, aesthetic, artistic, literary, philosophical and juridical traditions. This was made possible by what Jacques Gernet termed by the "prerogative of the written word in the Chinese world" --which was a "cultural and administrative language" and the "most effective instruments of political unification", playing the role of "recording and transmitting facts and ideas, which gives man a hold over space and time" and facilitated by intellectuals with "knowledge of writing and to book knowledge".

Book II continues with the Zhou dynasty's history (Chapters 24-26) and ends with chronicling of history of the Qin dynasty (Chapters 24-26), and Han dynasty plus the wars against the Huns (Chapters 29-41), up to Han Emperor Zhangdi (Liu Da, reign A.D. 76-88), with the A.D. 85 adoption of the *Sifen-li* posterior quarter remainder calendar serving as a convenient "semibreve rest". In regards to the Huns, Gernet had a brilliant reading of the Han dynasty chronicles to understand what China's colonial policy was really about, pointing out that "of ... ten milliards (i.e., 1 billion coins' equivalent revenues of the Han dynasty), three or four were absorbed every year by the annual gifts to foreign peoples", including 100,900,000 *ch'ien* (coins) to the southern Hsiung-nu in A.D. 91 and 74.8 million to the western territories. This is exactly the same bribery work as today's idiotic "Belt & Road" policy of Communist China. Note that Gernet hedged himself in pinning the Hunnic-Han War, namely, Emperor Liu Bang's defeat at the Baideng mountain, to the period "201-200 B.C.", which should be November 201 B.C. when strictly observing the *Zhuanxu-li* calendar's ordinal months. This author, having expanded the coverage of the Han dynasty bribery to the Hsien-pi, intends to expand the writings on the Huns to include a series of books on the other groups of barbarians in the future, like the Hsien-pi, the Turks, the Khitans, the Jurchens, the Mongols, and the Manchus.

In *Book II*, Chapters 37 and 38 are dedicated to interpreting *Shan Hai Jing* (The Legends of Mountains and Seas), with conclusion that the mountains' part was actually the ancient Shi-fa stalk divination, and the seas or overseas' components shared similar contents as seen in the divinatory books *Lian-shan Yi* (divination on concatenated [undulating] mountain ranges) and *Gui-cang Yi* (returning-to-earth storage divination), including the Wangjiatai excavated divination texts of the 3rd century B.C. and the materials from the Ji-zhong tomb excavation of A.D. 279. The one-hand and one-eye 'shen-mu-guo' (the deep eye socket) state, which was speculated to be the legendary one-eyed state Arimaspi that was described by Herodotus in *Histories* as located north of Scythia and east of Issedones, was debunked as having origin in the one-eye bird in the northern mountain range of *Shan Hai Jing*, and the one-eye and three-tail 'huan' foxlike animal on Mt. Yiwang-zhi-shan in the western mountain range of *Shan Hai Jing*. Not to mention having nothing to do with the pineal gland, or the eye of providence, or the eye of Horus. *Book II* has discourses on the Hundred Schools of Thoughts (Chapter 38) and the authenticity of *Shang-shu* (Chapter 41). Zhou China, i.e., what Hucker termed by China's formative age, left behind a legacy of the Hundreds of Schools of Thoughts, i.e., prolific academic and philosophical traditions that could be traced to Confucius and his disciples per Qian Mu, including Confucianism, Taoism, Mohism, Legalism, Nominalism, Syncretistism, Dialecticism, Naturalism, Mercantilism, and Egoism, etc. Gernet believed that Zou Yan (Tsou Yen)'s cosmological conceptions could be influenced by ancient India or Bactria, the Warring States' sophistry could be influenced by the Graeco-Roman oratory, and the Chinese school of sophists or dialecticians had the trace of the West, i.e., ten paradoxes equivalent from Greek philosopher Parmenides. Listing a purported East-West-shared Greek metaphor of the still shape of flying birds, Su Xuelin (1897-1999) claimed that Zou Yan (Tsou Yen), who propagated the Nine Greater Prefecture cosmology, must be a Central Asian or Western person; and that the Ji-xia academy of the Qi state, i.e., Plato's Peripatetic School Lykeion equivalent school, was staffed by the Westerners, not reconciling the fundamental difference between the Sinitic versus Greek theories on forms of matter. The Sinitic theory possessed five forms of matter, i.e., wood, mud, water, metal and fire, which were different from the Greek philosophical elements of earth, water, air, and fire.

So far, this *Introduction* devoted the majority of its passages to the highlights that underlie the factual theme of the duology *The Sinitic Civilization*. In here, the main purpose, reasons or motivation of this author's writing would not be expanded other than to repeat what was already mentioned in *Preface To the Second Edition* to *The Sinitic Civilization*. As to the "intended readers" of this duology, the author already pointed out in the second preface that "the two books were not intended for the serious-minded readers alone". This author, who likened the exertion of lifelong efforts to writing the two books to similar painstaking works by Zheng Sixiao (1241-1318), Wang Fuzhi (1619-1692) and Gu Yanwu (1613-1682), i.e., adherent loyalists from the alien conquest of China, hopes that readers of the duology on *The Sinitic Civilization* could generate and share the same innermost nostalgic sentiments about the ancient world. In the chapter on the authenticity of ancient version *Shang-shu* (remotely ancient history; book of documents), this author expressed wish that the debates about its authenticity would not be perpetual. For the post-Confucius Confucian Classic *Shang-shu*, it is important to bear in mind that the buzz words like '*de*' for virtues, '*ming*' for mandate, '*zhong*' for golden mean, and '*dao*' for way carried different connotation in different historical contexts. As to the forgery contemporary version of *The Bamboo Annals*, this author hopes that Professor Shaughnessy and the others in the academic world would express concurrence one day that the contemporary version of *The Bamboo Annals* was indeed a complete forgery inside and out. A separate publication on *The Bamboo Annals* with line-item rebuttals could be released. It is this author's hope that this duology could have rectified the Chinese history to its original truth that had been damaged by Qin Emperor Shihuangdi's book burning of 213 B.C. and that this duology could have expounded the Chinese tradition, humanity, culture and legacy to the world community.